Debbie H
In associati
& **Park Theatre** present

The
Retreat

By Sam Bain

Directed by Kathy Burke

G.
Lɪ
naɪ

The Retreat was first presented at Park Theatre on 2 November 2017.

The Retreat

by Sam Bain

Cast

TARA	Yasmine Akram
LUKE	Samuel Anderson
TONY	Adam Deacon

Creative Team

Director	Kathy Burke
Designer	Paul Wills
Lighting Designer	Paul Keogan
Sound Designer	John Leonard
Assistant Director	Siobhan James-Elliott
Producers	Debbie Hicks
	& Jesse Romain

Cast

Yasmine Akram | TARA

Yasmine trained at RADA.

Television credits include: *Sherlock, Lovesick, Stella, Undercover, Asylum, Unforgotten, The Centre, Damned, Metal Heart, Action Team.*

Presenting credits include: *Irish In Wonderland.*

Writing credits include: *Irish Micks and Legends, 10 Dates With Mad Mary, War Paint.*

Samuel Anderson | LUKE

Theatre credits include: *State Red* (Hampstead Theatre); *The History Boys* (National Theatre/US tour/Broadway); *Talking Loud* (Latchmere Theatre).

Film credits include: *Genesis, The Lady in the Van, Pleasure Island, Betsy & Leonard, Highlight, The History Boys.*

Television credits include: *Witless 1, 2 & 3, Trollied 4, 5, 6 & 7, Christmas Special, Loaded, DCI Banks, Moving On 7, Doctor Who, Death in Paradise, Bedlam, Midsomer Murders, The Big Picture* (Pilot), *The Job Lot* (Pilot), *Casualty, Doctors, Emmerdale, Gavin and Stacey, Stuck, Totally Frank, Hex, Doctors, King Crusades, Ramesses II: Mystery in the Valley of the Kings, Wannabes.*

Radio credits include: *The History Boys.*

Short film credits include: *Prodigals, Christmas Bonus.*

Adam Deacon | TONY

Theatre credits include: *East Is East* (West Yorkshire Playhouse/Octagon Theatre, Bolton/Theatre Royal, York); *Wasted, Cracked, Playing God, Where's Your Head At, Dear Danny Dilemma* (Y Touring Theatre); *Playing Fields* (Soho Theatre); *Mad Blud* (Stratford East); *House of Agnes* (Ovalhouse).

Film credits include: *To Dream, Montana, Comedown, Outside Bet, Payback Season, Anuvahood, Everywhere & Nowhere, Jack Falls, Outside Bet, Victim, 4321, Bonded by Blood, Shank, Adulthood, Wilderness, Sugarhouse Lane, Kidulthood, Don't Stop Dreaming, Ali G In Da House, Face, Fever Pitch.*

Television credits include: *Casualty, Suspects, Babylon, In Deep, Inside No. 9, Gates, Phoneshop, The Royal Bodyguard, Criminal Justice 2 Grownups Gunrush, Being Human, Deadset, West Ldn 10, Dubplate Drama, Ghost Squad, The Bill, Brief Encounters, Sugar Rush, A Touch of Frost, Is Harry on the Boat?, Passer By, Spooks, Wall of Silence, London's Burning, Spaced 2, Goodness Gracious Me.*

Creatives

Sam Bain | Writer

Together with Jesse Armstrong, Sam Bain has co-created and co-written nine series of the Channel 4 sitcom *Peep Show* from 2003–2015. *Peep Show* has won two British Comedy Awards, two Royal Television Society Awards, a BAFTA and the Writers Guild of Great Britain Award for Comedy Writers of the Year.

In 2011 Sam and Jesse created *Fresh Meat*, a team-written comedy-drama about university students, which won two RTS awards and a British Comedy Award. In 2014 Sam and Jesse wrote *Babylon*, a six-part hour-long comedy-drama series for Channel 4 and the Sundance Channel. The feature-length pilot was directed by Danny Boyle.

The duo's film writing includes 2010's *Four Lions*, co-written with Chris Morris, which premiered at Sundance and won the BAFTA for Outstanding Debut. Sam's first solo series, three-part comedy thriller *Ill Behaviour*, screened on BBC2 and Showtime in 2017.

Sam adapted his novel, *Yours Truly, Pierre Stone*, for a four-part Radio 4 series broadcast in 2017.

Kathy Burke | Director

Kathy Burke has worked extensively as director, actor and writer enjoying considerable success in each of the disciplines. Kathy won Best Actress at Cannes (1997) and a BIFA Award for *Nil By Mouth*; a British Comedy Award (2002) for *Gimme Gimme Gimme* and an RTS Award for *Mr Wroe's Virgins* (1994).

Recent film work includes: *Absolutely Fabulous the Movie*; *Pan*; *Tinker Tailor Soldier Spy*.

Kathy is well known for her TV work which includes: *Walking and Talking* which she wrote and acted in as 'the Nun'; *Ab Fab*; *Gimme Gimme Gimme* and several series of *Harry Enfield and Chums* and the spin-off film *Kevin and Perry Go Large*.

Writing credits include the award-winning stage play *Mr Thomas* which was later televised and a little cracker for Sky called *Better Than Christmas* which led to a spin-off four-part series called *Walking and Talking*.

Theatre directing includes: *Mr Thomas* for the Old Red Lion, which Kathy also wrote; *Out in the Open* by Jonathan Harvey (Hampstead Theatre); *Betty* by Karen McLachlan (Vaudeville Theatre); *Kosher Harry* by Nick Grosso (Royal Court Theatre); *Born Bad* by Debbie Tucker Green (Hampstead Theatre); *The Quare Fellow* by Brendan Behan (Oxford Stage Company); *Love Me Tonight* by Nick Stafford (Hampstead Theatre); *Blue/Orange* by Joe Penhall (Sheffield Crucible and tour); *The God of Hell* by Sam Shepard (Donmar Warehouse); *Smaller* by Carmel Morgan (Lyric Theatre, London); *The Stock Dawa* by David Eldridge (Hampstead Theatre); *Once a Catholic* by Mary O'Malley (Tricycle Theatre). She will be directing Oscar Wilde's *Lady Windermere's Fan* opening at the Vaudeville Theatre in January 2018.

Paul Wills | Scenic & Costume Designer
Theatre includes: *Measure for Measure* (Theatre For A New Audience, NY); *American Buffalo, Di and Viv and Rose, Mrs Henderson Presents* (West End/ Toronto); *King Lear, First Light* (Chichester Festival Theatre); *King Kong, Shakespeare in Love* (The Fugard Theatre, Cape Town); *Hamlet, The Two Gentlemen of Verona* (RSC); *Running Wild* (Regent's Park Open Air/ Chichester/UK tour); *Anna Christie, Making Noise Quietly, The Man Who Had All The Luck, The Cut, Novecento* (Donmar Warehouse); *Blasted, Saved, Punk Rock, The Chair Plays* (Lyric Hammersmith); *The Acid Test, Routes, Breathing Corpses* (Royal Court Theatre); *Richard II, Dr Faustus, Front Line* (Shakespeare's Globe); *Occupational Hazards* (Hampstead Theatre); *Our Few and Evil Days, Drum Belly* (Abbey Theatre, Dublin); *A Room with a View, A Steady Rain, The Hypochondriac* (Theatre Royal Bath); *Juno and The Paycock* (Gate Theatre Dublin); *A Human Being Died That Night,* (Hampstead Theatre/ The Fugard, Cape Town/BAM); *Howie The Rookie* (Dublin/The Barbican/ BAM); *Once a Catholic, Pornography, The Field* (Tricycle Theatre); *A Number, Total Eclipse* (Menier Chocolate Factory); *My Fair Lady, Afterplay, Sisters, Gladiator Games* (Sheffield Theatres); *The Indian Wants The Bronx* (Young Vic); *Finding Neverland, Buried Child, Barnum* (Leicester Curve); *The Changeling* (ETT); *Orpheus Descending 1984, Macbeth, See How They Run* (Royal Exchange Theatre, Manchester).

Opera and dance credits include: *Bastard Amber* (Liz Roche, Dublin Dance Festival); *Rusalka* (English Touring Opera); *The Magic Flute* (National Theatre of Palestine).

Paul Keogan | Lighting Designer
Paul was born in Ireland and studied drama at Trinity College Dublin and Glasgow University.

Credits include: *Jenufa, La Bohème, Eugene Onegin, Idomeneo, Les Dialogues des Carmelites* (Grange Park Opera UK); *Falstaff* (Vienna Staatsoper); *Far Away, Sacrifice at Easter* (Corcadorca, Cork); *The Gaul* (Hull Truck Theatre); *Maria de Buenos Aires* (Cork Opera House); *Sinners, Here Comes The Night* (Lyric Theatre, Belfast); *Blue/Orange, Tribes* (Crucible Studio, Sheffield); *Born Bad, The Stock Da'wa* (Hampstead Theatre); *Smaller* (West End); *Observe the Sons of Ulster Marching Towards the Somme, The Plough and The Stars, Cyprus Avenue, Shibboleth, Our Few and Evil Days, The Risen People* (Abbey Theatre, Dublin); *The Fairy Queen* (RIAM Dublin); *Powder Her Face* (Teatro Arriaga, Bilbao); *Wake* (Nationale Reisopera, Netherlands); *Novecento* (Trafalgar Studios, London); *Big Maggie* (Druid, Galway); *The Matchbox* (Galway International); *A Streetcar Named Desire* (Playhouse, Liverpool); *The Birds* (Gate Theatre, Dublin); *The Walworth Farce* (Landmark, Dublin); *Giselle, Sceherazade, Lost* (Ballet Ireland); *Flight* (Rambert); *No Man's Land* (English National Ballet); *Cassandra, Hansel and Gretel* (Royal Ballet).

John Leonard | Sound Designer

John Leonard has written an acclaimed guide to theatre sound, is the recipient of Drama Desk, LDI Sound Designer of The Year and USITT Distinguished Career Awards and is a Fellow of The Guildhall School of Music and Drama and an Honorary Fellow of The Hong Kong Academy of Performing Arts.

His most recent theatre includes: *All Our Children* (Jermyn Street Theatre); *Consent, Waste, Detroit, Grief, Untold Stories-Cocktail Sticks, 2000 Years, England People Very Nice, Much Ado About Nothing, London Assurance, Rocket to the Moon* (National Theatre); *The Heresy of Love* (Royal Shakespeare Company); *The Dark Earth and The Light Sky, The Master Builder, Little Eyolf, Ghosts* (Almeida Theatre/West End/New York); *Long Day's Journey Into Night* (Bristol Old Vic); *Into The Woods* (Royal Exchange Theatre, Manchester); *The BFG* (Birmingham Rep); *Birthday, Tribes* (Royal Court Theatre); *Stevie, Farewell to the Theatre, Lawrence After Arabia, Ken, Mr. Foote's Other Leg* (Hampstead Theatre); *Macbeth* (Shakespeare's Globe); *The Libertine, Dead Funny, Hand To God, The Duck House, Just Jim Dale, Firebird, McQueen* (West End).

Siobhan James-Elliott | Assistant Director

Siobhan graduated with a First Class BA Honours in Drama from the University of East Anglia in 2016. She is a Trainee Resident Director at the King's Head Theatre and will be assisting Adam Spreadbury-Maher on *La bohème* at Trafalgar Studios this December. Other recent directing credits: *Rubber Ring* (UK tour); *Hamlet* (assistant to Christopher Geelan, Young Shakespeare Company); *Half a Person* (UEA Drama Studio); *The Vagina Monologues* (The Studio, Norwich); *The Laramie Project* (UEA Drama Studio). Producing credits: *A Haunting* (Belgrade Theatre); *Coming Clean, 5 Guys Chillin'* (King's Head Theatre).

Siobhan also facilitates theatre for young people, previously at the Huntercombe Hospital Norwich, and currently assists with the National Theatre Young Technicians.

PRODUCERS

Debbie Hicks

Debbie is a theatre producer and manager working independently to deliver projects in the West End, off-West End, and on tour in the United Kingdom and internationally. She regularly collaborates with other theatre practitioners and producers, including Tom O'Connell. Debbie previously worked for Jamie Hendry Productions, where she trained as an apprentice under the Stage One initiative for new producers. She is also a postgraduate student of the University of Oxford and a member of the Society for Theatre Research. Recent credits include: *Out of Order* (UK tour); *Million Dollar Quartet* (UK tour); *North of the Sunset* (in development); *Dinner With Friends* (Park Theatre); *Holes* (Arcola Tent); *Shakespearience* (UK tour). For Tom O'Connell: *The Boys in the Band* (UK tour/West End); *Babe, the Sheep-Pig* (UK tour); *Raising Martha* (Park Theatre); *Loot* (Park Theatre/Watermill Theatre). For Jamie Hendry: *Impossible* (West End/international tour); *Let It Be* (West End/international tour); *Neville's Island* (West End); *The Wind in the Willows* (in development).

Jesse Romain

Jesse is an independent film and theatre producer. Plays include *Then Again* (Underbelly); *Mini-Break* (Underbelly and The Gatehouse) and with Debbie Hicks, *Holes* (The Arcola). He recently co-produced the short film *Edmund the Magnificent* and begins an MA in Film and Television Producing at The NFTS in January 2018.

General Manager	Debbie Hicks
Production Manager	Simon Streeting
Costume Supervisor	Mary Charlton
Assistant Costume Supervisor	Esme Kirk
Company Stage Manager on Book	Adam Moore
Assistant Stage Manager	Emily Humphrys
Set built by	Set Blue Scenery
Lighting provided by	Chauvet & TSL Lighting
Sound provided by	Purple Sheep
Marketing Consultant	Beth Nichols
PR	Mark Senior
Production Photography	Craig Sugden
Production Insurance	Lin Potter for WrightSure
Production Electrician	George Bach

The Producers would like to thank the following individuals and organisations without whom this production would not have been possible:

Michael Barfoot, Tom Basden, Ray Cooney, Jamyang Buddhist Centre, Dennis Kelly, Cathy King, Oliver Mackwood, Zoe Moore, Tom O'Connell, Ben Power, Jim Rastall, James Seabright, Andrew Treagus, Ryan Walklett, Tom Wilkes, Michael Maris (BUCK), Giggs and Danae'o

About Park Theatre

Park Theatre was founded by Artistic Director, Jez Bond. The building opened in May 2013 and, with three West End transfers, two National Theatre transfers and ten national tours in its first four years, quickly garnered a reputation as a key player in the London theatrical scene. In 2015 Park Theatre received an Olivier nomination and won The Stage's Fringe Theatre of the Year.

Park Theatre is an inviting and accessible venue, delivering work of exceptional calibre in the heart of Finsbury Park. We work with writers, directors and designers of the highest quality to present compelling, exciting and beautifully told stories across our two intimate spaces.

Our programme encompasses a broad range of work from classics to revivals with a healthy dose of new writing, producing in-house as well as working in partnership with emerging and established producers. We strive to play our part within the UK's theatre ecology by offering mentoring, support and opportunities to artists and producers within a professional theatre-making environment.

Our Creative Learning strategy seeks to widen the number and range of people who participate in theatre, and provides opportunities for those with little or no prior contact with the arts.

In everything we do we aim to be warm and inclusive; a safe, welcoming and wonderful space in which to work, create and visit.

★★★★★ 'A five-star neighbourhood theatre.' *Independent*

As a registered charity [number 1137223] with no public subsidy, we rely on the kind support of our donors and volunteers. To find out how you can get involved visit **parktheatre.co.uk**

Staff List

Artistic Director | Jez Bond
Executive Director | Rachael Williams
Creative Director | Melli Marie
Development Director | Dorcas Morgan
Development Assistant | Daniel Cooper
Finance Manager | Elaine Lavelle
Finance & Administration Officer | Judy Lawson
Sales & Marketing Manager | Dawn James
Deputy Sales & Marketing Manager | Rachel McCall
Venue and Volunteer Manager | Ehti Aslam
Technical Manager | Sacha Queiroz
Deputy Technical and Buildings Manager | Neal Gray
Cafe Bar General Manager | Tom Bailey
Administrator | Melissa Bonnelame
Learning Care & Access Coordinator | Lorna Heap
Duty Venue Managers | Barry Card, Shaun Joynson, Lorna Heap, Amy Allen

Bar Staff | Sally Antwi, Gemma Barnett, Florence Blackmore, Grace Botang, Calum Budd-Brophy, Robert Czibi, Jack De Deney, Nicola Grant, Adam Harding-Khair, Philip Honeywell, Lasse Marten, Jack Mosedale, Ryan Peek, Mitchell Snell, Temisar Wilkey, Leena Zaher

Box Office Supervisors | Sofi Berenger, Celia Dugua, Natasha Green, Holly McCormish, Jack Mosedale and Alex Whitlock

Public Relations | Julia Hallawell and Nick Pearce for Target Live

President | Jeremy Bond

Ambassadors
David Horovitch
Celia Imrie
Sean Mathias
Tanya Moodie
Hattie Morahan
Tamzin Outhwaite
Meera Syal

Associate Artist
Mark Cameron

Trustees
Andrew Cleland-Bogle
Nick Frankfort
Robert Hingley
Mars Lord
Sir Frank McLoughlin
Nigel Pantling (Chair)
Victoria Philips
Jo Parker
Leah Schmidt (Vice Chair)

With thanks to all of our supporters, donors and volunteers.

King's Head Theatre
The Future of the Fringe is here

About Us

The King's Head Theatre is proud to be an Associate Producer of *The Retreat*.

The King's Head Theatre was established in 1970. The most ethically and socially responsible fringe theatre in the UK, we are known for our challenging work and support of young artists. Last year 87,031 audience members saw a show of ours: 43,857 at our 110-seater home on Upper Street and 43,174 on tour. At our home in Islington we had 861 performances last year of 84 different shows.

We are committed to fighting prejudice through the work we stage, the artists and staff we work with and by producing work for minority audience groups. We believe in fair pay for all on the fringe and create accessible routes for early career artists to stage their work; work we are passionate about.

In 2019, we will move to a new permanent home in Islington Square, securing the future of the venue for generations to come.

As a registered charity (no. 1161483) with no public funding, we are incredibly grateful for the generous support of our Supporters and Friends who help us to make our vision of the future of the fringe happen.

Resident Trainee Directors

At the heart of our commitment to providing opportunities for emerging artists sits our resident trainee director's scheme. Founded in 1994, it won the Queen's Jubilee Award in 2002 in recognition of its unique value to the arts.

Our ambition is to give directors all the practical skills they need to direct, produce and manage their own work. The trainees spend 12 months with us; they are allocated to in-house productions as assistant directors, producers and stage managers and receive weekly skills and learning sessions with a range of external industry professionals. For this production of *The Retreat*, the assistant director, Siobhan James-Elliott, is one of our resident trainee directors.

Our Team

Artistic Director | Adam Spreadbury-Maher
Executive Director | Fiona English
Senior Producer | Louisa Davis
Producer | Oscar French
Theatre Manager | Bex Foskett
Production Manager | Pete Foster
Office Manager | Alan Stratford

Resident Trainee Directors
Ben Anderson
James Callàs Ball
Siobhan James-Elliott
Eloïse Poulton

Associate Artists
Harry Mackrill
Becca Marriott
Benji Sperring

Junior Associates
Jamie Armitage
Ellen Buckley
Mike Cottrell
Jennifer Davis
Catherine Éxposito
Helena Jackson
Dave Spencer

Board of Trustees
James Seabright (Chair)
Tahmid Chowdhury
Yasmin Hafesji
Mary Lauder
Amanda Moulson
Heather Ruck
Molly Waiting
Richard Williamson

We are grateful to our Supporters, Friends and wider community of donors who are crucial to ensuring our continual support of emerging companies and exciting, ethically made fringe work. To find out more about how you can support the home of fringe theatre visit www.kingsheadtheatre.com

THE RETREAT

Sam Bain

For Wendy

Characters

LUKE
TONY
TARA

A one-roomed stone hut in the Scottish Highlands. Evening turning to night outside.

The set is laid out on the flat/thrust stage, the only wall being the back wall, the other three are empty space.

Against the back wall (upstage left) there is a single bed with meditation cushions in a neat pile at its foot and a large poster of a Tibetan Buddha on the wall above it.

Next to the bed is a bedside table and there is a shelf on the wall above it decorated with Tibetan prayer flags. The shelf contains a few Buddhist books and a statue of Green Tara.

Further along is a gas heater, a stove, and a table with cooking implements, plates, etc. There is a small window in the wall above the table (upstage centre).

There is a door at the back of the hut, and a threadbare armchair on the other side of it (upstage right). There is a stool in the corner of the room (downstage right).

At the front of the stage a small shrine has been set up – a low rectangular wooden table with candles, water bowls and wax flowers in front of a golden Buddha statue (downstage centre). There is a Tibetan singing bowl on an ornate cushion next to the shrine.

LUKE *is kneeling in front of the shrine. He is in his thirties. He is clean shaven, has a crew cut and is dressed in practical outdoor wear – a maroon fleece, hiking socks.*

He is holding a small porcelain jug of water. There's a row of eight small bowls on the shrine. Five are already full of water, the other three are upside down.

He turns over the sixth bowl and very carefully fills it with water, then places it back on the shrine. He does the same with the next two bowls.

He puts the empty jug on to the floor, takes out a box of matches and carefully lights the three candles on the shrine.

He blows out the match then takes a white cloth from a cardboard box on the floor nearby. He carefully removes a (branded) chocolate bar from inside the box and places it on the shrine.

Then, facing the shrine, he walks back several paces. He puts his hands together in 'prayer position' at his chest, closes his eyes for a beat.

He opens his eyes and moves his hands together up to his forehead – then down to his throat – then back to his chest – then drops to his knees, puts his palms on the floor in front of him and puts his forehead on the floor, lifting his palms above his head. Then he gets to his feet, goes back to his starting position. He completes the prostration three times.

Then he crosses to the meditation cushions and places them carefully in the centre of the room. He sits on the cushions, facing the shrine.

He takes a wooden stick and strikes the rim of the singing bowl, creating a distinctive tone which rings out.

After a beat he picks up a mala (Buddhist rosary beads), places it in his left hand. He starts to chant, counting each mantra with the click of a bead as he does so:

LUKE. Om mani padme hum – Om mani padme hum – Om mani padme hum

The door quietly opens and TONY *enters.* TONY *is also in his thirties, dressed in more urban clothing and carrying a rucksack. He has a scarf and hat on.*

Om mani padme hum – Om mani padme hum – Om mani padme hum

TONY *quietly approaches* LUKE *and watches him for a moment.* LUKE *doesn't notice him, he's so deep in concentration.*

Om mani padme hum – Om mani padme hum – Om mani padme hum

After a beat TONY *quietly steps further inside the hut. He goes over to the bed – looks through the books on the shelf.*

Om mani padme hum – Om mani padme hum – Om mani padme hum

Then he goes over to the kitchen area. Looks through the cooking implements.

TONY *picks up a container of metal spoons – then deliberately drops the spoons on the stone floor, making a loud noise.*

LUKE *leaps up in shock, turns round.*

(*Freaked.*) Aaaaahhh!

TONY (*mock-freaked*). Aaaaaaahhhhhh!

LUKE (*scared*). I haven't got anything, take it all!

TONY. Cheers, but I've got enough spoons as it goes.

TONY *takes off his hat and scarf, revealing his face.*

LUKE. Tony??

TONY. Just thought I'd pay you a little visit. You don't mind do you? It's been too long.

LUKE. How – how did you get here?

TONY. Train to Glasgow, bus to Inverness, hitched. Then when I finally got here I had to walk up a fucking mountain and get past your bouncers – a couple of baldy monks in purple robes.

LUKE. Didn't you think about – phoning ahead?

TONY. I did – last week. They said I couldn't talk to you, or even leave a fucking message.

LUKE. They're not supposed to disturb me while I'm on retreat.

TONY. What if it's important?

LUKE. I guess they have to make a judgement on how important it is…

TONY. Right, and you told them: 'if it's Tony, it's definitely not important – in fact make sure you tell him to go fuck himself.'

LUKE. No, I never even mentioned you actually.

TONY. It is important, as a matter of fact. Really important. Yeah, I've got news. Big news.

LUKE. Right?

TONY. The thing is… I don't know how to say this… but… it's – Raymond.

Beat.

Raymond's dead.

LUKE *takes this in.*

It happened last week. He had a stroke. Brain haemorrhage. Totally out of the blue. He was in hospital for about five days and then – that was it.

LUKE. Right.

Beat – then:

Who's – Raymond?

TONY. Dad's uncle. Uncle Raymond.

LUKE. Oh right. In Canada?

TONY. Yup.

LUKE. Didn't Dad used to call him Ray?

TONY. Raymond, Ray – what does it matter? The point is, he's dead.

LUKE. Right.

TONY. Yeah. It must be a bit of a shock.

LUKE. Was he, in pain when he died, or…?

TONY. I dunno. I didn't get a chance to actually see him. I mean he's in Canada, so.

LUKE. Right.

TONY. So. The funeral's next week.

LUKE. Okay.

TONY. Vancouver. It's about ten hours away. But it's off-season, so we could get tickets pretty cheap.

LUKE. Okay. Normally, of course I'd come… but right now it's difficult. I'm kind of – busy.

TONY. Doing what?

LUKE. My retreat. It's a three-month retreat on compassion. I've still got over a month to go, so…

TONY. You're so busy being compassionate you can't go to Uncle Ray's funeral?

LUKE. We never actually met him.

TONY. Yeah we did.

LUKE. When?

TONY. When he came over, that Christmas.

LUKE. When we were kids?

TONY. Yeah.

LUKE. I don't remember.

TONY. Well, I do. He gave me a water-powered rocket.

LUKE. Right? And that was a big deal for you?

TONY. I only used it once and it didn't work. Well, it did, if you wanted to re-enact the Space Shuttle disaster. But it was a nice thought.

LUKE. Maybe you could – represent me at the funeral?

TONY. Represent you? Like your lawyer? What do you expect me to tell them? 'Sorry, Luke couldn't make it. There was some urgent sitting needed, and there wasn't anyone else available with an arse.'

LUKE. I can be more help to Ray staying here than I could by watching his body being burned.

TONY. Help him? It's a bit late for that.

LUKE. There's still time to do a powa for him…

TONY. A what?

LUKE. Powa. P–O–W–A. It's a special ceremony us Buddhists perform when someone's died. It takes seven to ten days after death for the very subtle mind to leave the body. As long as you perform the powa before then, it can make all the difference.

TONY. Make what difference?

LUKE. You chant a mantra to purify the person's negative karma and help them towards a fortunate rebirth. It's one of the kindest gifts you can give.

TONY. Just for the record, I'd prefer some Quality Street or a cake.

LUKE. A cake won't be much use to you once you're dead.

TONY. And a 'powa' would be?

LUKE. Absolutely.

TONY. So if I died, you'd sit around for hours praying for my soul?

LUKE. Yes.

TONY. That's really annoying.

LUKE. You'd be dead.

TONY. Exactly. I won't be around to tell you what a dick you're being.

LUKE. Look, I appreciate you coming all this way to see me, but…

TONY. '…but I'm sitting on my arse getting high on my own supply, so piss off and leave me alone'?

LUKE. That's not what I'm saying.

TONY. Well, that's what I'm hearing.

LUKE *starts tidying up the mess* TONY *made*. TONY *looks around*.

Not a nice place you have here.

LUKE. It's not meant to be five star, it's designed for retreat…

TONY. 'Retreat.' Isn't that what an army does when it's losing?

LUKE *blows out the shrine candles, clears away the cushions*.

LUKE. It's kind of a – spiritual holiday.

TONY. You're having a nice holiday. That's nice.

LUKE. So you got the postcard?

TONY. Yeah. Is that a new phrase for when you screw someone over? 'I gave him the postcard.' 'Yeah, I totally gave him the postcard.'

TONY *takes a postcard from his pocket*.

LUKE. No, obviously I…

TONY. There was me sitting around like an idiot thinking 'he'll be back any day now'. Then I get 'the postcard'. 'Starting retreat, please pay bills and redirect post.' They don't charge you per word, you know.

LUKE. I wanted to keep it – to the point.

TONY. Yeah well, you managed that pretty successfully.

Beat.

In other news, I broke up with Annie.

LUKE. Oh I'm sorry. I didn't know you two were… having trouble.

TONY. Well, I didn't get a chance to talk to you about it, did I? Before you ran off.

LUKE. I didn't 'run off'.

TONY. What would you call it? You just – disappeared. It was like you'd kidnapped yourself.

LUKE. I just needed to – get away.

TONY. From me?

LUKE. No.

TONY. So what did I do?

LUKE. You didn't 'do' anything – it just – the flat wasn't a, a positive environment. There were a lot of... distractions.

TONY. What – you mean me and Annie? I guess we could be a little bit noisy, sorry about that. You could have turned up your stereo.

LUKE. I got rid of my stereo.

TONY. You could have borrowed my stereo.

LUKE. Knocked on your door mid-shag and asked to borrow your stereo?

TONY. That's what living with people is like. Fucking pain in the arse. But you just have to deal with it.

LUKE. I think I'm just the sort of person who prefers living alone.

TONY. No kidding.

LUKE *starts sweeping the floor with a broom.*

LUKE. It wasn't just the noise. It was the drugs, the booze. I just needed a break.

TONY. Maybe I needed a break too. Did you ever think about that? We could have gone away somewhere together.

LUKE. I wanted to do something spiritual.

TONY. We could have found somewhere spiritual that also has a nightclub?

LUKE. I don't think we would have found somewhere like that.

TONY. I bet the Hindus don't mind if you shake your booty.

LUKE. I really wouldn't know.

TONY (*after a beat*). You know what you need? A girlfriend.

LUKE. Oh really?

TONY. You don't need Buddha, you need to wake up with someone else's hand on your knob for a change.

LUKE. Grinding your genitals against somebody else's isn't the answer to all life's problems.

TONY. I know you had a shitty marriage. But that doesn't mean you should write off the whole female race.

LUKE. They're not a race.

TONY. Sorry?

LUKE. Women aren't a race. They're a gender.

TONY. That's pretty racist.

LUKE. It's really not.

TONY. Look, I know you and Lisa had some big ugly fights. Shit happens.

LUKE. I don't know what you...

TONY. I saw that cut on her face.

LUKE. It wasn't... I didn't cut her face. I just – threw a pillow at her.

TONY. You must have thrown it pretty hard.

LUKE. She was holding a glass at the time. I didn't mean to...

TONY. You don't have to explain. The only reason I never sent Annie to the hospital is my aim's no fucking good.

Beat.

Listen. Women are mental. One minute you think she's the missing piece of the jigsaw, the next you want to plough her face in with a steam iron. You've just got to stick it out, then you get to the good stuff.

LUKE. What good stuff? You leaving them, them leaving you, watching them die or them watching you die?

TONY. Are you seriously saying there's no point in trying cos one day it's all going to end?

LUKE. The end of meeting is parting. The end of collection is dispersion. The end of rising is falling. The end of birth is death.

TONY. In that case, what's the point of doing fucking anything?

Beat.

Anyway. I brought a bunch of stuff I thought you might need. Is that all right, or do I have to run it past the prison guards?

TONY *opens his rucksack.*

Speakers for my phone. Couple of books – Ian Rankins. Your favourite. Some of those posh olives you love, a fuck-off Toblerone…

LUKE. That's really kind. But I'm doing a semi-fast for the retreat. I'm not eating anything after lunch.

TONY. Well, if you're not eating, you still have to drink.

TONY *takes out a can of lager from the bag.*

Stella Artois. 'Reassuringly alcoholic.'

TONY *throws* LUKE *the lager,* LUKE *catches it and immediately puts it down on the table.*

LUKE. I'm fine, thanks.

TONY. Tell you what – fancy a bit of a pick-me-up?

TONY *takes out a bag of coke, offers it to* LUKE.

LUKE. Er… no.

TONY. Oh go on.

LUKE. No thanks.

TONY. Why not? You used to love it.

LUKE. That was a long time ago.

TONY. No it wasn't. It was like, last year.

> TONY *pursues* LUKE *around the room with the coke.*

> Come on, man, it's premium grade, this ain't no pub grub!
> Get it up there! This'll get you higher than squatting on that
> arse cushion.

> LUKE *slaps* TONY*'s hand away, the coke spills on the floor.*

> Shit! Now look what you made me do! There's dust and crap
> all over my gear. Give me a dustpan and brush. And a sieve.

LUKE. For God's sake…

TONY. That's a hundred quid's worth of coke. Give me a
hundred quid or give me a dustpan and brush and a sieve.

> LUKE *gives* TONY *a dustpan and brush and a sieve.*
> TONY *starts sweeping the coke into the dustpan, sieving
> out the dirt.*

LUKE. I take it you never went back to rehab.

TONY. I don't need rehab. I can stop whenever I want.

LUKE. You tried stopping before.

TONY. I *succeeded* in stopping.

LUKE. But you started again.

TONY. I decided to stop. And then I decided to start again.

LUKE. What about NA?

TONY. The catch with NA is, they want you to stop taking drugs.

> TONY *finishes sweeping up the coke. He carries the dustpan
> full of coke to the bed, starts sieving it into a saucepan.*

I know I was a bit out of control before, but I've got a rule now – I only drink or take drugs when someone else is around.

LUKE. Even if the other person's not taking them? Even if they were shouting 'Tony, Tony, don't do it!'? Does that still count?

TONY. Fuck off. Look if I'm an addict, so are you. Except I've got coke and you've got your stupid cushion.

LUKE. You can't compare drugs and meditation.

TONY. I was there, mate. When you quit your job and started sitting on the floor with your eyes shut eight hours a day. If I told you you couldn't meditate again, you'd freak out just as much as if you were a crackhead and I took away your crack.

LUKE. Being a Buddhist's nothing like being a 'crackhead'. It's a completely different kind of high. High's the wrong word, I meant…

TONY. If you think you can get just as out of it by meditating, you've taken the wrong drugs, mate. Why climb the stairs when you can take the lift?

LUKE. Because the lift sometimes crashes and you die?

Beat.

We'll just have to agree to disagree…

TONY. I'm not 'agreeing to disagree'.

LUKE. Okay then let's just disagree.

TONY. Face it. You're hooked on this shit just like you were hooked on work.

LUKE. I wasn't 'hooked' on work. You have to work long hours in the City. It's stressful and competitive. That tends to be the case in jobs where they pay you a lot of money.

TONY. Yeah, but you loved it didn't you? First in, last out. I remember you coming in after you'd pulled an all-nighter, you were high as a kite, like you'd taken four E's instead of been crouched over a computer for twenty-four hours…

LUKE. If you'd ever had a job beyond riding around on your pushbike, you might understand.

TONY. It's not a 'pushbike' it's a Pinarello FP3 Centaur with a full-carbon monocoque frame, and I'm not 'riding', I'm delivering.

LUKE (*after a beat*). What do you want, Tony? You didn't come all the way here just to invite me to a funeral and give me some chocolate.

TONY. Why the hell else would I come to this shithole?

LUKE. To see me?

TONY. And I suppose wanting to see my own brother, that's a crime all of a sudden?

LUKE. If you're worried about me, don't. I'm fine.

TONY. Yeah but you're not though, are you? You're riding the magic banana up the beanstalk to fairyland. Someone's got to try and bring you back down – pop the bullshit balloon.

LUKE. This an 'intervention' isn't it? Except your idea of an intervention is trying to shove coke up my nose.

Beat.

Why don't you just go?

TONY. Fine by me. Why don't you come with me?

LUKE. Because I've got a retreat to finish.

LUKE takes out his meditation cushions.

TONY. Don't tell me you're going to meditate now.

LUKE. I'm going to finish the session you interrupted.

LUKE sits on a meditation cushion.

He strikes the singing bowl, then picks up the mala.

He places his hands one on top of the other on his lap, and closes his eyes.

TONY. Oh for fuck's sake.

TONY clicks his fingers in front of LUKE*'s face. No response.*

TONY plugs his iPhone into the speakers, starts playing dance music at top volume.

TONY starts dancing. Dances around the room, singing along to the track.

Ooh Luke, Luke…

Still LUKE *doesn't react.* TONY *stands to the side of* LUKE *and unzips his flies.*

If you don't stop meditating, I will put my penis in your ear. That is going to happen.

TONY zips up his fly. Walks away. Sits on the bed, starts eating the chocolate bar.

LUKE *leans over, turns off the music.*

Must be hard. Being all on your own up here. No phone, no internet. No hookers, just boring monks and nuns.

LUKE *looks alarmed.*

Yeah, I know all about the hookers. I saw the bills, man. 'EG Services.' Great website they have as it goes…

LUKE. You opened my post??

TONY. You had an account. You were probably getting hooker Nectar points.

Beat.

I couldn't believe how much you were spending. Once a week, twice a week, three times – and top drawer – prime porky-worky. No bargain-bucket pussy for you…

LUKE. I'm not discussing this. You stole my private information…

TONY. What, I didn't have a search warrant, so it doesn't count?

LUKE. Look… I…

Beat.

It's an issue, okay? It *was* an issue. But I've dealt with it.

TONY. What, by being here?

LUKE. Yes, by being here.

TONY. It must be easy to stop banging hookers when there aren't any hookers around to bang.

LUKE. I'm purifying my mind.

TONY. Yeah right.

LUKE. It was – part of the whole, work/City thing – that's all in the past.

TONY. I don't think even your most hardcore desk-jockey mates were banging prozzies three times a week.

LUKE. It's behind me. I'm a Buddhist now.

TONY. You've been born again, in the church of blue balls?

LUKE. I'm focusing on real love, real compassion…

TONY. At some point you're going to have to come down off your mountain. And when you do, there'll be hookers. And they'll be just so pleased to see you.

LUKE. Maybe I won't come down off my mountain then.

TONY. What's that supposed to mean?

TARA (*offstage*). Jamyang? Jamyang?

LUKE. H-hello?

The door opens and TARA enters. She is painted head-to-toe in green body paint, including a third eye in the middle of her forehead, and is dressed in silken robes and jewellery, including a tiara – and wrapped in a body warmer jacket. She is carrying a small box of food.

TARA. Hi – it's just me…

LUKE. Oh – hi!

TARA. Oh – sorry. I didn't realise you had a guest…

LUKE. This is my brother, Tony. Tony, this is – Tara.

TARA. Good to meet you.

TONY. The pleasure's all mine.

TARA (*to* LUKE). I think the monks dropped your food box off at my hut. There must have been a mix up – it's got dairy stuff in it.

TARA inspects another food box just inside the doorway.

Yeah, this one looks like mine…

TONY. 'Jamyang' – what's that? Buddhist for hello?

TARA. No, it's…

LUKE (*quickly, covering*). It's more like a nickname. My Tibetan nickname. Like Tara's is – Tara.

TARA. My real name's Daisy, but everyone calls me Tara.

LUKE. Green Tara's a Buddhist deity.

Gestures to statue.

She's doing a Green Tara retreat, chanting a hundred thousand mantras.

TARA. I'm doing a tantric visualisation where I imagine myself transformed into Green Tara. It kind of helps to dress like her. Sort of like – Buddhist cosplay?

TONY. Tantric, eh? Sounds like my kind of meditation.

TARA. It's not sexual. Tantra's a way of challenging our view of self as solid and fixed.

Beat.

Sorry, I'll let you get on with your visit…

TONY. No no no, stay – take a seat.

LUKE. Tony's not staying.

TONY. I would have taken off already but Luke begged me not to. We haven't seen each other for ages, he really wanted to catch up.

(*To* TARA.) How about a cup of tea? Go on.

(*Irish accent – like Mrs Doyle from* Father Ted.) Go on, go on, go on.

(*To* LUKE, *explaining.*) *Father Ted*. Cos she's Irish.

TARA (*laughs*). Er. Sure – why not?

TONY (*to* LUKE). Put the kettle on, mate. Make us one while you're at it.

LUKE *hesitates, then crosses to the kettle – touches it.*

LUKE. I'll just warm this up.

LUKE *slips on a pair of hiking sandals and exits.*

TONY (*after a beat*). You know, I think what Luke's doing is incredible.

TARA. That's great. Most muggles don't understand retreat – they think you're giving something up.

TONY. But really you're gaining something.

TARA. Exactly!

Beat.

Usually people have been meditating a lot longer than Luke before they do a retreat on their own.

TONY. Well, he's not entirely on his own is he?

TARA. I guess my hut isn't far away…

TONY. No, I mean – cos the Buddhas are with him, guiding him on his spiritual journey.

LUKE *enters with some wood, puts it in the stove and turns it on. Looking over at* TONY *and* TARA *suspiciously.*

TARA (*to* TONY). So what do you do? In London?

LUKE *looks at the saucepan full of coke on the floor under the window.*

TONY. Deliveroo. But not for much longer. I'm writing a screenplay. It's a British gangster movie. But the twist is – no guns. These guys solve their problems with the power of their minds.

TARA. Great.

LUKE *picks up the saucepan, tips the coke out of the window.*

TONY. I haven't had time to finish it though – all I seem to do is bloody work.

TARA. That's London for you. That's one of the reasons I moved up here.

TONY. Right. Yeah. For real.

Beat.

So you guys met at that hippy festival in Ireland?

LUKE. Yeah. Last summer.

TARA. Luke walked into my meditation tent.

TONY. And it was love at first sight.

LUKE *and* TARA *look uncomfortable.*

What I meant was, that's when he fell in love with meditation. Right, bro?

LUKE (*sharply*). Yeah 'bro'.

TONY (*to* TARA). That was *your* festival, right? You ran it. 'The Daisy Chain'.

TARA (*surprised*). Er, yeah, that's right. Did Luke mention…?

TONY. I did a bit of googling.

TARA (*on the back foot*). Right?

LUKE. You've been spying on her?

TONY. Googling, mate. Not spying. Googling. Just wanted to know who my brother was shacked up with. In a manner of speaking.

(*Beat, to* TARA.) It wasn't doing too well, was it, by the end? Your festival.

TARA (*uncomfortable*). Well, we had some – cashflow issues. The margins started getting too tight. We were the first festival in County Offaly then bloody 'Castlepalooza' started and hoovered everyone up... it's hard to compete with a castle, you know what I mean?

TONY. No, sure. Of course.

TARA. 'Castlepalooza' isn't even a word. Just adding 'palooza' to something doesn't make it a word.

TONY. Couldn't agree more, mate. Couldn't agree more.

Beat.

Well, I think it's great, what you're doing here – the Buddhist centre. It's great to meet someone who isn't afraid to do something they really believe in, something...

TARA. Weird?

TONY. I wasn't going to say 'weird'.

TARA. I'm wearing green body paint and a tiara. I'm comfortable being weird.

TONY (*after a beat*). So – up here with the monks and the nuns – you must get... lonely...

LUKE *eyes* TONY *hard as he brings over the teas.*

TARA. Not really.

TONY. You're not exactly the spinster cavewoman type.

LUKE (*happy to be interrupting – to* TONY). White, one sugar.

(*To* TARA.) Camomile.

TARA. Thanks, Luke.

(*Then, to* TONY.) I've had pretty much all the sex I've wanted to have, if that's what you're talking about.

TONY. So you're out for the count? Retired undefeated?

TARA. More like a shop that's closed for refurbishment.

After a beat, TONY *crosses to the iPhone speakers.*

TONY. Fancy some music?

LUKE. I think we're fine, thanks.

TONY *starts playing a dance track.*

TONY. Bet neither of you have partied for a while.

TARA. You'd be right about that.

TONY. Let's have a party then. Buddha's not like Jesus, nailed to a plank, giving everyone a massive downer. Buddha wants you to have a good time, all of the time.

TONY *starts dancing.* TARA *laughs.*

LUKE *crosses, turns off the music.*

Oi!

LUKE. My house, my rules.

TONY (*to* TARA). It must feel great, being the one who got Luke into Buddhism.

TARA. I really don't think I can take credit for that...

TONY. Sure you can. He wouldn't have gone anywhere near a meditation cushion if he hadn't been dazzled by your – obvious, spiritual, assets.

LUKE *glares at* TONY.

Sometimes I wonder if it's really Buddha he's trying to impress with all this self-denial?

LUKE. What would you know about Buddha?

TONY. He's just teasing. We've been talking Buddhism ever since I got here.

TARA. Yeah? And you reckon you're – converted?

TONY. Totally. When Luke started to explain it, it was like a window opened in my soul. Or I should say – my 'very subtle mind'.

TARA (*not buying it*). What do you love about it?

TONY. I just love – the inner peace. Karma. Future lives. Who wouldn't want to have lots of future lives? Like being Doctor Who without all the Daleks.

LUKE. So you're basically a Buddhist now?

TONY. Er, yeah. Basically. Yeah. I would say so.

LUKE. You sure you don't want a beer to wash down that tea, Tony?

(*To* TARA.) Tony loves his beer!

TONY. Nah, I'm all right thanks.

LUKE. That's amazing. Truly, that goes to prove the enormous power of the Buddhas and Bodhisattvas. Cos what was it you were saying half an hour ago? 'This Buddhist shit' – something like that?

TONY. No. Nothing like that.

LUKE. No, that's what you said. I remember it quite clearly. It was just before you tried to shove cocaine up my nose.

TONY. That's funny.

(*To* TARA.) He's actually very amusing when he tries.

LUKE. It's true. He spilt it all over the floor. Right there.

TONY. Yeah, well, you know, I just fancied a bit of a pick-me-up. Anyway, the point is, I came to see him because our uncle just passed away.

TARA. Oh – I'm sorry…

LUKE. Great uncle.

TARA. I was with my granddad last year when he died. I got to do a powa in the same room. I really don't think it could have been any more perfect.

TONY. Yeah. My dog died recently – it was amazing.

TARA. It was an incredible teaching to spend time in the room with him after he died.

TONY. You're a cheap date, aren't you?

TARA. Death meditation is actually really powerful. Focusing on the fact that I could die at any time, it just makes all my tiny problems that much tinier.

LUKE. Death's an 'inconvenient truth'.

TONY. You two are like a walking warning of what happens if you don't have a telly.

LUKE. There's a great story from Buddha's life. A woman begged the Buddha to bring her dead son back to life. He agreed – but only if she collected a mustard seed from every house in the village that had never been touched by death. She agreed, and went to knock on every door in the village – but came back empty-handed.

TONY. So Buddha played a practical joke on someone whose son just died. Nice. What else did he ask her for, a left-handed screwdriver?

Beat.

Death doesn't bother me. I'll go out with a bang. Do a *Thelma and Louise* – drive off a cliff in a Cadillac, tripping my nuts off, getting a blow job from a supermodel.

TARA. Talking to you is like talking to a teenager.

TONY. I can't help it if I'm a funny guy.

LUKE. What he means is, he can't have a serious conversation without making a joke.

TONY. Course I can. It's just not as much fun, is it?

TARA. So… you came all the way up here to tell Luke he had a death in the family.

TONY. Yup.

TARA. Why didn't you just phone, or send him a letter?

TONY. I tried.

LUKE. Not that hard.

TONY. It's the kind of news you need to break in person.

TARA. I remember Luke said your parents both died when you were young. Did it bring back any of those memories?

TONY (*uncomfortable*). Er, yeah. Sort of.

TARA. That must have been a really hard time.

TONY. Er, yeah. I guess it was.

TARA. No wonder you and Luke are so close.

TONY (*unsure*).…yeah.

TARA. When something like that happens you must really have to rely on each other.

TONY. Yeah.

TARA. You must really need each other.

TONY. I kneed him in the balls once if that's what you mean…

LUKE. The truth is, Tony came up here to do an intervention on me.

TONY. I just wanted to know what the hell's going on in his head.

LUKE. You wanted to tell me that I'd lost my mind.

TONY. I just wanted to know if you were actually serious.

LUKE. Of course I'm serious.

TONY. You say that, but…

(*To* TARA.) You know what we used to call Luke when he was a kid? Mr Changey-Mind. Cos he changed his mind the whole time. He'd take up football for two weeks when the World Cup was on, then when it was Wimbledon he'd be Andre Agassi – headband and everything.

TARA (*amused*). Is that right?

TONY. Mum and Dad used to indulge him, I guess cos he was the youngest, you know, the golden boy. So they'd buy him all this expensive stuff – football boots, tennis rackets – and after a couple of weeks he'd get bored of it and it'd just lie around and rot.

LUKE. That's not true.

TARA. Your parents sound really nice.

TONY. Yeah, if you were Luke. They wouldn't even buy me a bike.

LUKE. They bought you loads of bikes, you just kept losing them.

TONY. I didn't lose them, they got nicked. There's a difference.

LUKE. They bought him a brand new BMX for Christmas – two hundred quid. And the first day he took it out he chained it to a pole that wasn't really a pole…

TONY. It was a pole.

LUKE. Okay, it was a pole but it was like – this high.

Demonstrates about six feet.

And there was nothing at the top of it! So whoever nicked it just lifted it over the top!

TONY. It was an easy mistake to make.

LUKE. And then he went crazy when they wouldn't buy him another one!

TONY. If they'd got it insured, it wouldn't have been an issue.

LUKE. You were seventeen, you could have got it insured yourself.

TONY. Yeah but I didn't, did I?

Beat.

Anyway, the point is, I'm normal and you two are freaks.

TARA. And that makes everything all right? Being normal? Even though you're miserable, better not try anything different in case you look like a freak.

TONY. If I thought you were doing something proper I might be able to take you more seriously. If you were for real you'd be in Tibet or India, not bloody Scotland.

TARA. That's like saying because you really like spaghetti you should move to Italy.

TONY. Yeah. Well, you should.

TARA. Buddhism isn't something you have to learn from a book, or a teacher. It's something you do. Every day should be a meditation. Eating can be a meditation. Walking can be a meditation.

TONY. Shagging?

TARA. Of course. Why not?

TONY. Sign me up for your advanced shagitation course.

LUKE. The point is, it's a mindful way of life. And it's a lot easier to live mindfully somewhere like this than back in crazy London or mental India...

TONY. You're just having a gap year fifteen years too late.

TARA. Maybe you'll feel differently after Luke gets ordained.

TONY. Gets what?

TARA (*realises – to* LUKE). You haven't told him?

LUKE. Uh. No. Not exactly.

TONY. Tell me what?

LUKE. I'm – going to – take vows to become a monk.

TONY. You're going to become a *monk*? Like those weirdos outside??

LUKE. Uh, yes. The ordination ceremony's at the end of my retreat.

TONY. No, you didn't tell me that. I think I would have remembered that.

LUKE. I would have mentioned it before but…

TONY. But you didn't want to spoil the surprise?

Beat.

So next time I see you you'll be wearing a purple dress?

LUKE. Robes. Purple robes.

TONY. Oh my God. The buzz cut. I thought it was to stop the midges nesting but it's a practice hairdo isn't it? It's like you've got heels on before you go full drag!

LUKE. There's a lot more to ordination than a haircut. I'll be given a new Tibetan name…

TONY. Jamyang. Your 'nickname'.

LUKE. Yes. And I'll take vows. I should be able to remember them all, we were studying this… 'to abandon killing, stealing, sexual conduct, lying and taking intoxicants, to practise contentment, reduce the desire for worldly pleasures, abandon engaging in meaningless activities, maintain the commitments of refuge and practise the three trainings of pure moral discipline, concentration and wisdom.'

TONY. 'Sexual conduct' – meaning sex?

LUKE. Trust you to focus on that one.

TONY. No sex? Ever again?

LUKE. That's right.

TONY. Fucking hell.

TARA. Looks like you two have some… stuff you need to talk about. I'll see you later.

(*Aside to* LUKE.) Let's have a chat later, yeah? I'm around.

LUKE. Tara…

TARA *exits*.

TONY. Jesus fucking Christ. A monk. You're going to be a *monk*.

Beat.

When were you planning on telling me?

LUKE. I don't know. I hadn't decided when I was going to tell you – or anyone.

TONY. If I hadn't come up here I wouldn't even have known. You'd probably have Skyped me for the next twenty years wearing a wig.

Beat.

Fucking unbelievable. I mean I knew you were into this shit but I had no idea you were this far gone.

Beat.

Why are you doing this? Cos the Sexy Shrek told you to?

LUKE. Tara didn't even…

TONY. You want to be the golden boy at the head of the class. You want to please Mummy, get an apple for teacher, get a pat on your baldy head.

LUKE. I'm doing it because I want to do it, because it's the right thing to do. The most amazing opportunity to get fast-tracked to enlightenment.

TONY. A new name. Fucking hell. What's wrong with your old name? Our name?

LUKE. There's nothing wrong with it, it's just… I'll be a new person. So I'll need a new name.

TONY. Why do you have to be a new person? What's wrong with the person you already are? I mean you're a prick and everything, but... can't you just be yourself? Can't you just think for yourself?

LUKE. Thinking for myself wasn't really working out for me.

TONY. So you'd rather join a cult? That's pathetic.

LUKE. It's not a cult.

TONY. And you're in a good position to judge that, are you?

LUKE. You belong to a cult more than I do.

TONY. How'd you work that one out?

LUKE. The cult of 'looking out for number one'. The real rebels are people like Buddha who go against the mainstream – materialism, secularism... You take the piss out of me for bowing to a shrine, but you bow too – at the shrine of cool. You don't prostrate to Buddha, you prostrate to... the Fonz.

TONY. 'The Fonz'?? That's your ideal of 'cool'? 'The Fonz', in his leather jacket?

LUKE. Okay, not the Fonz. Robbie Williams or...

TONY. *Robbie fucking Williams??*

LUKE. You know what I mean.

TONY. You know what, I don't. I haven't got a clue what you're on about. You had a great job, loads of money – and you want to piss it all up the wall – for this?

LUKE. I had all that stuff, but it didn't make me happy.

TONY. Happy? What right have you got NOT to be happy? When there are... junkies in the Philippines collecting sparkplugs off landfills? Little kids in Africa walking round with no legs?

LUKE. Are you saying I should be happy cos I've got legs?

TONY. What have you got not to be happy about anyway? Apart from being here. But you chose to be here, so that doesn't count.

LUKE. There are millions of people who haven't found happiness through worldly success and turned to the spiritual path. Buddha started life as a prince in a palace. Or someone like George Harrison, who had all the fame, money and adulation imaginable but…

TONY. Are you comparing yourself to George Harrison now?

LUKE. Only in the sense that I was successful but…

TONY. George Harrison was in The Beatles, man. *The Beatles*. You ran a firm of investment consultants.

LUKE. All right, fine, I'm not George Harrison.

TONY. So that's it? In a couple of months the shears come out – off go the bollocks? You're just – giving up?

LUKE. I'm not 'giving up'…

TONY. Yes you are. You're giving up on life.

LUKE. I'm giving up on suffering. I'm giving up on samsara and moving towards a deeper, more meaningful way of life…

TONY. Just cos you haven't had much luck with women doesn't mean you have to throw in the towel.

LUKE. What's so noble about carrying on with the endless boxing match of 'romantic love' – otherwise known as 'deluded attachment'?

TONY. Why do you have to piss all over everything?

LUKE. You've hardly got a relationship history to boast about. You've lurched from one nightmare woman to the next…

TONY. Maybe, but I've had a hell of a lot of fun in the process.

LUKE. Celibacy sounds weird, but the amount of time and energy and – peace you get back when you're no longer engaged with the impossible task of trying to keep someone else happy… it might sound like death to you, but really it's a burst of new life.

TONY. Oh come on, man. Don't put your pecker in the deep freeze yet. You've obviously got a hard-on for Tara…

LUKE. That's… that's not the case, that's not the case at all.

TONY. Pause before denial. Case closed.

LUKE. The case isn't 'closed', I was just pausing before I…

TONY. Case closed!

LUKE. Will you stop saying 'case closed'?! The case is not closed!

There's absolutely nothing going on between us. We're both here for the same reason…

TONY. Fucking and sucking.

LUKE. To study and meditate.

TONY. You met her at a festival, you were on the rebound, pissed and stoned probably, and you fell for her. There's no shame in that. She's smoking hot, I don't blame you…

LUKE. That's not what happened.

TONY. You fell in love with someone – fucking wicked.

LUKE. No I didn't.

TONY. But it all got a bit too much. It's scary when someone actually gets close, isn't it? So you'd rather activate the ejector seat. Vertical take-off into la-la land. I bet you hope she gets ordained too, right? Mr Monk and Mrs Nun – perfect cop-out marriage. No arguments about kids or the mortgage, just one long celibate brainfuck.

Beat.

No sex – I take it that means no kids, right?

LUKE. No.

TONY. Jesus, man. Having kids – that's the whole point isn't it?

LUKE. Well, it's an excellent way to distract yourself from the fact you're going to die. But unfortunately the distraction only lasts eighteen years. After that you're just the same as you were before, but eighteen years closer to death.

TONY. You don't become a real man till you're a dad.

LUKE. You don't become a real man till you have sex and forget to wear a condom?

TONY. There's a lot more to being a dad than that.

LUKE. Except in your case.

TONY. Fuck you. I'd do anything for Natasha. It's not my fault her mum's a total bitch.

LUKE. Because she doesn't like it when her daughter walks in on you screwing some random meth-head?

TONY. Once! I did that one single time! And she wasn't a 'meth-head', she was a casual meth user.

Beat.

And it's not my fault Tasha doesn't know how to knock.

LUKE. Look. I'm not saying having kids isn't great. In fact I'm sure it's wonderful. It's the only taste of the bliss of unconditional love most people will ever get. But why limit your experience of unconditional love to one or two people? Why not expand it to include the whole world? Not just your kids, family and friends but everyone – colleagues, acquaintances, strangers – the postman…

TONY. The postman?

LUKE. That's an example.

TONY. Are you saying you have unconditional love for your postman?

LUKE. Well, I try to. That's the ideal…

TONY. Why have kids when you've got a postman? Is that what you're saying?

LUKE. In a sense, but…

TONY. You should tell him. Your grizzled Scottish postie with the lunchbox full of haggis. Tell him you love him unconditionally. Maybe put it in a letter? It's a format he understands.

LUKE. People have children because they think it'll make them happier. But what if they're wrong? What if they're still just as miserable, but now they've got a couple of vulnerable little humans to take care of? How happy are those little humans likely to be? Or doesn't that matter? Is that just 'collateral damage'?

TONY. You've never been a parent, you don't know what the fuck you're talking about.

LUKE. Do you think having kids made Mum happier? If anything it just made her drink more.

TONY. So you're saying she shouldn't have bothered? You'd rather she never went to all the hassle of creating you?

LUKE. No. I mean yes, of course. I mean…

TONY. If you regret being born, why don't you just jump then? End it all?

Beat.

Is it because you already have? Becoming a monk is just a glamorous way of killing yourself. Luke is dead, long live Jamyang.

LUKE. I thought about it, all right?!

TONY. About what?

LUKE. Ending it all.

TONY. When?

LUKE. Last year.

TONY *takes this in as* LUKE *goes over to wash up the tea mugs.*

It was all getting a bit too much. The divorce. The… the hookers. Work. I didn't actually quit my job, you know. They gave me my marching orders. 'Compassionate leave.' They could see the wheels were coming off. My own company. The company I'd built. Telling me I couldn't hack it. The worst thing about it was, they were right. I wasn't sleeping, I was making mistakes…

Beat.

I felt like I'd failed. Marriage, career – everything. I had some sleeping pills from the doctor's. Had a good, hard look at them. But I didn't do it. I flushed them. And stopping work ended up being the best thing that could have happened. I went to that festival, started meditating. It saved me. It saved my life.

Beat.

So you've got a choice – between a Buddhist brother and a dead one.

TONY. You could have talked to me, bro.

LUKE. Could I?

TONY. Yeah, you could.

Beat.

So what's the plan then – after the monk-over?

LUKE. My plan is to stay here and carry on with my studies.

TONY. So when are you planning on coming home?

LUKE. I'm not.

TONY. You're going to stay up a mountain for the rest of your life, sitting on your arse thinking about how great you are?

LUKE. Well – nothing's permanent.

TONY. What?

LUKE. Buddhist joke. About impermanence being the nature of things.

TONY. Oh. Right. Ha ha.

LUKE. Look. The thing is – I was going to tell you… I'm actually… I'm going to sell the flat. I'm putting it on the market.

TONY. What? But – why? You don't need the money. You're living off half a carrot.

LUKE. The plan is, when it's sold, I'm going to give the proceeds to the centre.

TONY. You're *giving away* our flat?

LUKE. Well, yeah. But it's not going to affect you, immediately. You'll have plenty of time to find somewhere else to live…

TONY. Oh yeah, sure, that'll be no problem, me with my credit rating and my massive income, should be able to stroll in pretty much anywhere.

Beat.

Fucking hell. Do you even know how much that flat is worth?

LUKE. I've got a pretty good idea…

TONY. Go on. I want you to say it.

LUKE. Er – I guess – something like – nine nine four nine fifty? Approximately.

TONY. That's about right. You'll be giving away close to a million quid. To the jolly green giant and the skinhead losers.

LUKE. They're not… but, yes. Yes that's the, general plan.

TONY. Great plan. Brilliant plan. What a marvellous plan. Take a long time for Tara to come up with that plan, did it?

LUKE. It's not her plan – it's my plan.

TONY. Oh sure. Course it is. What the fuck is she going to do with it all anyway? I mean how many lentils can you eat?

LUKE. It's not for – food. It's for – the temple.

TONY. The what?

LUKE. Tara wants to build a temple. On land belonging to the centre.

TONY. She's building a temple? But she doesn't even own the place.

LUKE. Yes she does.

TONY. No, she doesn't. When I googled her, her company details came up – 'Daisy Kelly Limited'. Did you know you were in love with a limited company?

LUKE. I'm not…

TONY. Anyway, there wasn't any property listed under her assets. In fact her assets were fuck-all if I remember correctly.

LUKE. You must have made a mistake, it wouldn't be the first time.

TONY. Course not. Because I am a mistake, right?

Beat.

How much else has she raised for this temple?

LUKE. I don't think… I think the main, bulk of the cash is going to come from the flat sale.

TONY (*starts laughing*). This gets better and better.

LUKE. Look, most of the people who are living here are students or in the caring professions – teachers, nurses…

TONY. Losers. No-marks.

LUKE.…and most of the monks and nuns don't work at all…

TONY. Course they don't. Why work when you can live off handouts from a clueless mug? They must love you!

LUKE. I'm just in a very fortunate position, to be able to help…

TONY. Oh yeah. Very fortunate. Lucky, lucky old you.

LUKE. There wasn't any coercion, any pressure…

TONY. Right. No pressure.

LUKE. In fact Tara didn't say yes immediately, she wanted me to think about it deeply…

TONY. That was nice of her. Was this before or after she put on her lovely costume?

LUKE. That has nothing to do with it.

TONY. The fact that you want to give her all your money has nothing to do with the fact that you're desperate to fuck her?

LUKE. I don't want to – do that. But even if I did, it wouldn't have anything to do with it.

TONY. She's playing you like a monkey with a barrel organ. You're a wallet in a purple robe. Of course she wants you to get ordained – monks don't have annoying wives and kids hoovering up all their cash, do they?

Beat.

I'm looking out for you here…

LUKE. Sure you are.

TONY. It's obvious you want to fuck her. I know. She knows. Buddha knows. Everyone knows. Because a) you obviously do and b) who wouldn't? I would. As long as I had some white spirit to get the green paint off my cock afterwards.

LUKE. For God's sake…

TONY. Don't you think Tara might be teasing your todger a little bit? Making it go hard so it nudges your wallet out of your pocket and spills a million quid?

LUKE. Tara's a good person. She doesn't want to exploit me, she just wants to benefit the whole world. It's not a cult…

TONY. *Not* a cult. Good to clear that one up. It's *not* a cult.

LUKE. It's *Buddhism*. It's one of the world's great religions.

TONY. Got that on her headed paper has she, when she comes begging for money?

LUKE. How do you think all the synagogues and mosques and Hindu temples in this country got built? They didn't just appear overnight. They were funded by people who followed the religion.

TONY. You've only been into this five fucking minutes!

LUKE. *A year.* Some people get married after less than that.

TONY. George Harrison didn't give up his mansion when he found enlightenment.

LUKE. No, and some nutter broke in and tried to kill him.

TONY. Your point being?

LUKE. That having a big house doesn't protect you from suffering.

TONY. Right now the only person who's going to try and kill you is me.

LUKE. I know this must be weird for you. But I've thought about it a lot, and this is what I want to do with *my* money. And *my* life.

TONY. What about my life?

LUKE. Well, obviously I want what's best for you…

TONY. If you want what's best for me, here's an idea – *don't sell my fucking home*.

LUKE. It's not personal. I'm not trying to hurt you. I'm just trying to do what's best.

TONY. And this is for the best, is it?

LUKE. I think so.

TONY. What the fuck do you even need a temple for?

LUKE. For meditations – teachings. A temple is like a hospital, for the mind.

TONY. It's a mental hospital? For the mental?

LUKE. No it's not, it's…

TONY. If you're so desperate to give your money away, give it to someone who needs it. Poor people – the homeless – beggars…

LUKE. It would actually be better if beggars gave money away rather than asking for it. That's the quickest way to purify their bad karma and create the cause for wealth in future lives.

TONY. What a wanker.

LUKE. Money's only a temporary fix anyway. Being rich doesn't stop you being miserable. People focus so much on outer happiness, but inner peace – peace of mind – that's real happiness.

TONY. Oh for fuck's sake.

LUKE. Think about it. We've got more and more wealthy, we're living longer and longer – but has it actually made us any happier?

TONY. Yes. Obviously. Of course it has.

LUKE. Do people look happy to you? When you get on the Tube, are you faced with a sea of smiling faces?

TONY. No. Because they're on the fucking *Tube*.

LUKE. Everyone says they're fine – but everyone you know well, really well – aren't they all just basically – fucked?

TONY. No. Jesus. What are you on?

LUKE. Everyone's just trying to get hold of some noise-cancelling headphones to block out the screaming coming from inside their heads and everyone else's.

TONY. And you've got the answer have you? Sitting up here on Mount Olympus with your food box?

LUKE. I'm just trying be happy, okay? I'm trying to find some – meaning to life.

TONY. 'The meaning of life'? What are you, fourteen? Just get on with it, like everybody else.

LUKE. Right. Just get on with it. Carry on working and eating and shitting and sleeping and watching TV and going on holiday and texting and having sex and talking and having a cup of tea and getting cancer and watching *Game of Thrones* and dying?

TONY. Yes. Brilliant. I mean what's your problem?

LUKE. My problem is – that's not enough for me! That's nowhere near enough. Borrowing money we don't have, to buy things we don't need, to get happiness that won't last.

TONY. Save me the sermon.

LUKE. The Buddhist path worked for me, there's no reason it couldn't work for everyone.

TONY. You reckon it's working for you do you? That's what you reckon?

LUKE. Yes. I've always had this – voice – in my head…

TONY. You can get treatment for that, you know. They do medication these days.

LUKE.…this voice in my head telling me I'm not good enough. No matter how hard I worked or how much money I earned, I could never shut it up. It just sat there like a parrot on my shoulder, shitting down my back. But it's gone now, and I've almost done cleaning up the parrot shit.

Beat.

It works, Tony.

Beat.

I remember the first time I meditated. I put it off for ages. I was scared – actually scared of just sitting down and – stopping! Just stopping this – rolling barrel of filth that's my mind…

TONY. Why stop it? Why not jump in and have a good wallow?

LUKE. The first silent retreat I did, it was like babysitting a radio DJ with attention deficit disorder. Blah blah blah blah – resentments about the past, fears about the future, what he thinks of me, how can I impress her? Just self-obsessed nonsense! And I realised – that was my life. Rolling downhill in this barrel of filth. All I'd been doing as far back as I can remember was chasing after 'the next big thing' – the 'big fix'. But as soon as I got 'the big thing', it was replaced by something else. When I was sixteen, losing my virginity was going to make everything all right. Then getting into uni was going to make everything all right. Then a good job was going to make everything all right. Then buying a flat was going to make everything all right. Then being in a relationship was going to make everything all right...

TONY. You should try snorting pure MDMA, that really does make everything all right.

LUKE. It was only in meditation that I made the amazing discovery that at the bottom of the barrel was this enormous well of inner peace and bliss. That's what the mind is really like! All the anger and craving and nonsense is just... shit on the surface of a diamond. You get rid of the shit and the diamond's there – just, perfect.

Beat.

By meditating you can get real, lasting happiness from a source you can really rely on. By helping to build a temple I've got an opportunity to share that with so many people...

TONY. Why do you care more about helping a bunch of strangers than you do about helping me?

LUKE. It's not one or the other – the temple won't just be for Buddhists, it's for anyone who wants to come...

TONY. I don't want to come.

LUKE. Well, that's your choice.

TONY. But getting kicked out of my home, that isn't my choice?

LUKE. Maybe this is for the best? Maybe this is just the incentive you need to really, you know – sort your life out.

TONY. Oh great. So this is all for my benefit? Fuck you 'Dad'.

LUKE. Well, I just think...

TONY. Oh yeah, this is just what I need. I'm doing a job I hate, I've just broken up with my girlfriend – wouldn't it be cool if I was also homeless? That's just the pick-me-up I've been looking for.

LUKE. You must admit you've been in a bit of rut the past few years. When you first came to stay with me it was just going to be for a couple of months. Two years later and…

TONY. Sorry, I didn't realise there was a time limit. I didn't realise there was a gun to my head.

LUKE. Not a gun, I just mean…

TONY. If you were a proper human being, you might actually think, 'ooh, I wonder if my last living relative might need some help before I spunk my entire wad all over a bunch of freaks?'

LUKE. The temple is an extraordinary opportunity to create good karma…

TONY. Karma. Brilliant. Take your head out of your arse. It's so far up there, you're wearing your intestines as a hat.

LUKE. Look – Tony. I feel bad – evicting you. It's just…

TONY. If you feel that bad, give me the flat.

LUKE. What?

TONY. If you're so keen to give the flat away, give it to me.

LUKE. Don't be ridiculous.

TONY. Not just for me – for Tasha.

LUKE. What's Tash got to do with anything?

TONY. I could take care of her better if I had money. I could, I don't know – pay for her to go to private school.

LUKE. I thought she liked her school?

TONY. Yeah but who knows, she might like a private school even better.

Beat.

Come on, man. Please. I need the money. Things are tight. Really fucking tight. I'm broke. I had to sell my bike.

LUKE. That's not my problem, that's…

TONY. But I'm kind of more than just broke, aren't I? Broke is when you've got no money. I've got less than no money. A lot less.

LUKE. Debts?

TONY. Yeah.

LUKE. You took out a loan?

TONY. Yeah. Well, not just the one loan. Lots of little ones.

LUKE. How much? In total?

TONY. A hundred thousand.

LUKE. You owe a *hundred thousand pounds*?!? Who to??

TONY. Remember the guy who used to sell me hash and weed? Bert.

LUKE. You owe a hundred grand to Bert??

TONY. He introduced me to this guy Nico who works in this hardware shop. We were mates for a while. I mean, not mates, he's a wanker, but he did this poker school on a Friday night...

LUKE. I'm sure if you arrange to pay in installments you can...

TONY. He's not exactly the The Listening Bank. He's got all these heavy mates. And he works in a *hardware shop*.

LUKE. So?

TONY. So he's got unlimited access to hardware. Drills, hacksaws, pipe wrenches...

LUKE. I'm sure he won't do – anything.

TONY. And you're prepared to take that chance are you? 'I'm sure he won't cut off your balls. Oh look, he cut your balls off. Sorry.'

LUKE. Just talk to him, explain that...

TONY. We already talked. This is his idea of talking. With a razor blade.

TONY *opens his shirt. There's a nasty scar on his torso.*

LUKE. How long has this been going on? Why didn't you tell me about it before?

TONY. Because you weren't around, were you? And because I wanted to sort it out on my own. But I couldn't, okay?

Beat.

I bet that makes you happy.

LUKE. It really doesn't.

TONY. If I don't get a hundred grand from somewhere, I'm going to lose a finger. Think you'll win a gold medal in the compassion Olympics, sitting up here in your temple while your brother loses a finger?

LUKE. You're not going to lose a finger.

Beat.

This is the real reason you came here, isn't it? To ask for money.

TONY. I came to see my brother.

LUKE. But you are also asking for money.

TONY. None of this would have happened if you hadn't taken off. You could have given me some advice – you're good with money.

LUKE. So it's my fault?

TONY. I know this is shitty for you, but I'm fucked. And I really need your help. You used to be a Marxist – 'to each according to his needs'...

LUKE. I was a Marxist when I was sixteen.

TONY. Oh yeah. After you were a Christian, before you got into martial arts, before you turned into a City boy, before you became Mr Dalai Lama. It's hard to keep track.

LUKE. I'm sorry you're in this situation. I hope you find a way out of it. But I'm not going to give you the money from the flat sale. It's mine. And it's spoken for.

TONY. You'd never have a fucking bean if it wasn't for me.

LUKE. How do you work that one out?

TONY. I was there at the beginning of your stupid 'consultancy'. It was my idea.

LUKE. Your idea?

TONY. When you were working at that bank with all those French wankers and you were pissed off with everything, and *I* said, 'Why don't you start your own company?' Remember? You never would have done it if I hadn't put the thought in your head first.

LUKE. I think I would have thought of starting my own company.

TONY. I bet you wouldn't have. It was my idea. And I helped start it. I helped build it up.

LUKE. You painted our first office. And I paid you.

TONY. Exactly. I was there at the beginning.

LUKE. You didn't even do a very good job. I had to get the carpets replaced cos there was paint all over them.

TONY. And I did the IT.

LUKE. You plugged in a few computers…

TONY. You didn't know your arse from a printer port before I turned up. I supported you. I encouraged you. I listened to you moaning on for hours about that dick you hired who pissed off to Israel with your database…

LUKE. Are you my wife?

TONY. Yeah, I sort of am, aren't I? I'm your first wife. The little woman in the attic you cut loose when you meet someone hotter – who in this case is a green chick.

LUKE. So because of all you've 'done for me' you think I owe you my flat?

TONY. Our flat.

LUKE. It's *not* our flat!

TONY. It's where we both live. But you want to keep it all for yourself. You're so selfish.

LUKE. *I'm* selfish? If I'm selfish, what does that make you?

TONY. I'm not the one going on about how unselfish I am. I'm not pretending I'm not selfish.

LUKE. Maybe you'd have your own flat right now if you hadn't spunked your inheritance up the wall?

TONY. I didn't 'spunk it up the wall'.

LUKE. All right, shoved it up your nose.

TONY. Fuck you. I made damn good use of it. I went to Mexico. I got a scuba diving certificate.

Beat.

Anyway it wasn't my fault, I got the money when I was too young…

LUKE. I was younger.

TONY. And the fact that you squirreled your share away in your Abbey National Savers account like some geek means you're a modern-day Jesus does it?

LUKE. No, it means I own a property and you don't.

TONY. Yeah well, it was a tough time, wasn't it? It was a fucking tough time…

LUKE. For both of us.

TONY. Yeah but it was tougher for me.

LUKE. No it wasn't.

TONY. It was. I was the oldest. Three bottles of wine and one car crash later – bang, head of the fucking family.

LUKE. No one had to be head of the family, it was just the two of us…

TONY. Yeah, the bad boy and the golden boy.

LUKE. What does that mean?

TONY. You know exactly what it means.

LUKE. Being the golden boy wasn't all roses, you know. Mum was all over me, it was like I couldn't breathe...

TONY. I wouldn't have minded a bit of that. A bit of attention would have gone a long way.

LUKE. You got to be independent, do your own thing, live your life.

TONY. In other words, they didn't give a shit about me?

After a beat, TONY *goes to the saucepan, opens the lid.*

Where's my coke?

LUKE. It's gone.

TONY. What do you mean? Where is it?

TONY *starts aggressively searching through* LUKE*'s stuff – first the kitchen area, then over to the bed –*

LUKE. You don't have to do that.

TONY. Yes I fucking do.

LUKE. You won't find it under there.

Before LUKE *can stop him,* TONY *lifts up the mattress and pulls out a magazine, holds it up – it's a porn mag.*

TONY. Oh my word.

Chuckles.

Look what we have here. *Fiesta.* Old-school. Brilliant.

LUKE (*opens eyes, embarrassed*). That's – private. That's, personal...

TONY. Yup. Very personal. You could have got something a bit classier – *Penthouse* or *Buddhist Babes.*

LUKE *goes to snatch the magazine out of* TONY*'s hand but* TONY *skips away out of reach.*

LUKE. It's not... it's none of your business.

TONY. The hookers are behind you, but these lovely ladies are very much still on the scene.

Flicks through the magazine.

Bet you like meditating on her long and hard.

LUKE. I haven't looked at it more than a couple of times...

TONY. I'm not judging you. I think it's great. There's hope for you yet. We all need to jerk off now and again.

LUKE. I was going to get rid of it before my retreat – I don't know why I even brought it...

TONY (*re: magazine*). I know why. Cos you couldn't resist 'trainee accountant Heidi''s lovely boobs and bush. Who could?

LUKE. Can you just – put it away now?

TONY. And she's a blonde, a *real* blonde. Nice. Plus she's *spiritual*. She's made for you, dude.

LUKE. Look, I'd really prefer if you...

TONY. '"I've always been interested in the wisdom of the East", says this striking saucepot. "I've done some chanting, and I tried out tantric sex – it lasted for hours!" For our money this horny knockout is definitely full of Eastern promise!'

LUKE. Could you just – put it away now, please?

TONY. You want to stop, just when it's getting real? This is the real you – the big hard dick poking through the Jedi trousers.

LUKE. This is *not* the real me.

TONY. Well, it's yours, and it's real, so I kind of think it is?

TONY *throws the magazine on to the bed.*

Guess the good thing about a monk's robes is they're nice and roomy. You'll be able to strap some porn mags round your waist like a sex mad suicide bomber. 'Friar Fuck, The Monk Full of Spunk.'

Beat.

You're so two-faced. It's all right for you to have your wank rag but you won't let me have my little bit of charlie. Where is it anyway?

LUKE. I got rid of it.

TONY. You fucking what?

LUKE. I threw it out of the window.

TONY puts his head out of window.

TONY. You owe me a hundred quid, mate!

LUKE. It's for your own good. It makes you edgy.

TONY. Where's that fucking sieve?

TONY picks up the sieve, takes out a little tube/pipe and snorts the coke residue from it. LUKE stares at him. TONY opens up a can of Stella.

Don't look at me like that. I'm not Mum.

LUKE. Why, cos she was hooked on booze and painkillers and you're hooked on booze and coke?

TONY. No – because I'm not a mental alcoholic fuck-up.

LUKE. She did the best she could.

TONY. It's all right to feel angry with her, you know.

LUKE. In the Sutras Buddha warned that a single moment of anger creates the cause for rebirth in the hell realms for a hundred thousand aeons.

TONY. And what does having a wank get you? Ten years with the devil's red hot dildo up your arse?

Beat.

The truth is, Mum was an alcoholic fuck-up and Dad was a spineless twat.

LUKE. You shouldn't say things like that.

TONY. What, you're worried I'll go to hell? Or are you more worried that you'll have to listen to some truth for a change?

Beat.

No wonder she picked you instead of him.

LUKE. Sorry?

TONY. He was a pathetic excuse for a husband so she married you instead.

LUKE. I think you should just stop talking now.

TONY. I remember being in the same room as you two. When you used to play those endless games of chess… I felt like a gooseberry on someone else's hot date.

LUKE. Shut up, Tony. Just shut up.

TONY. Ooh. Now we're getting somewhere. Can't get angry at lovely dead Mummy and Daddy but you can at bad boy brother.

LUKE. You're the one who's obsessed with all this, I've moved on, I've forgiven them…

TONY. No you haven't.

LUKE. Yes I have.

TONY. You can't give someone a pardon unless you've found them guilty first. It's like eating pudding before you've had your greens.

LUKE. What are they guilty of?

TONY. Being fucked up. Fucking us up.

LUKE. And that makes you feel good, does it? Blaming them for everything?

TONY *shrugs.*

All right, they were screw-ups and they screwed us up, I'm a screw-up, you're a screw-up, everyone's a screw-up –

Attenborough's a paedo, Judi Dench is a crack-whore –
happy now? Full of the joys of spring?

TONY. No.

LUKE. Exactly. Now we both feel like shit. Congratulations.

TONY. The truth isn't always feelgood but on the other hand,
it's the truth.

LUKE. Yeah well, you can take your 'truth' and just… just, go.

TONY. So you can get back to meditating on love and
compassion? It's a lot easier being loving and compassionate
when there's no one around, isn't it?

LUKE. Just go.

TONY. Maybe I will. Go back and change the locks.

LUKE. What?

TONY. You're not going to be able to sell the flat if you can't
get through the front door, are you?

Beat – LUKE *looks worried.*

And on the way I might stop off at Tara's. She's in a hut, on
her own, up a mountain… I bet she'd respond to a little
attention – know what I mean?

LUKE. You're just jealous. Cos you've never achieved anything.

TONY. Me – jealous of you?

LUKE. I've found something I love and you can't have it so
you want to break it.

TONY. You think I'm jealous of a twat who's so scared of life
he escapes to a hut? Who's so fucking angry with women he
can't have a relationship with one without almost killing
them? Whose idea of safe sex is a vow of celibacy?

LUKE. Fuck you.

TONY. Here it comes.

Laughs.

Finally. You dress up all spiritual, but really it's a front. A front for a cunt.

LUKE. You're the cunt.

TONY. All that meditation really did the trick, didn't it? You didn't just waste a year of your life or anything. No chance. This isn't just a big load of old bullshit, is it?

TONY kicks the shrine. Candles and water bowls fall off.

LUKE. What are you doing?!

TONY. No, that can't be true, cos if it was you'd have to come back down to earth with the rest of us dickheads...

TONY kicks the shrine again.

LUKE. Stop it!!

LUKE kneels to repair the shrine – touches the bowls and offerings to his 'third eye' on his forehead before putting them back.

TONY. Tell you what. I'll make you an offer.

Beat.

Half. Give half the flat to the Buddhists and half to me.

LUKE. That's not an offer. That's a demand.

TONY. Either way.

LUKE. Why on earth should I give you half my flat?

TONY walks to the kitchen area. Picks up a kitchen knife.

TONY. What if something happened to you? Something – bad. You know. *Terminally* bad. I'm your only living relative. I reckon I'd get the flat anyway.

TONY approaches LUKE, toying with the knife.

LUKE (*laughing*). Are you – threatening me? Are you threatening to *murder* me??

TONY. You don't think I've got the balls, do you? The question is – is it worth taking that chance?

LUKE. What are you saying?

TONY *approaches, points the knife at* LUKE.

TONY. I'm saying – do you feel lucky? Well, do you? Do you feel lucky, monk?

LUKE. Put the knife down.

TONY. Not laughing now, are you?

LUKE. If I was found dead, don't you think the police would want to have a chat with the brother who'd just inherited my flat? It's hardly the perfect crime.

TONY. I'd come up with an alibi.

LUKE. What about Tara? She knows you're here.

TONY. What if I got rid of her too?

LUKE. You're going to kill both of us? You're going to go on a *killing spree*?

TONY. Why not? And after I finish the job, I'll plant the knife on you. Knife in one hand, jazz mag in the other. She caught you having a wank, you stabbed her, then topped yourself.

LUKE. Go on then. Do it. I'm not afraid. I know where I'm going when I die.

TONY. Don't give me your Buddhist shit. I'm serious – if you don't give me the money I'll fucking do it!

LUKE. Dying on retreat guarantees rebirth in a pure land. Killing your brother, on the other hand, guarantees rebirth in a hell realm. It's your choice.

TONY *approaches* LUKE, *arms outstretched. They face off for a beat.*

Then TONY *drops the knife and grabs* LUKE. *They start having a messy fight.*

TONY (*laughing*). Just like old times, eh?!

LUKE *starts tickling him.*

LUKE. Remember that? Remember that?

LUKE starts whacking TONY playfully with a meditation cushion.

Meditate on that!

TONY (*laughing*). All right, all right – I give in!

Then the door opens and TARA appears. She's out of costume – just wearing outdoor gear.

TARA. Is everything all right?

LUKE (*embarrassed*). Oh – er – hi.

TARA. I heard – shouting?

LUKE. Uh – yeah. Yeah, everything's – fine. We were just – playing around.

TONY. Luke went for me.

LUKE. No I didn't! You tried to stab me!

TONY. Yeah right.

LUKE (*points*). He vandalised my shrine.

TONY. You beat up the heretic cos he kicked the idols?

LUKE. I didn't beat you up and they're not 'idols'. Anyway, you provoked me.

TONY. 'It wasn't my fault officer, he just wouldn't shut up.' That's you isn't it? Wife-beater Buddha. What you going to do next? Cut my face with broken glass?

LUKE. It was a pillow! She was holding a glass at the time…

LUKE gestures at his pillow – realises the porn mag is lying on the bed in full view. He quickly sits down on the bed – on top of the magazine.

(*To TARA.*) I'm sorry… you don't need to see any of this…

TONY. No, stay, he might not hit me again if you're here. You can be my 'human shield'.

LUKE. I thought you were going?

TONY. Yeah. Maybe I will. Go back to London and barricade myself in. Hello flat, goodbye temple.

TARA. Oh, so you told him about the temple?

TONY. Yeah, the donkey's out of the box.

(*To* TARA, *aggressive*.) You know what? I blame you more than I blame him. He's been brainwashed.

TARA. Luke's perfectly able to make his own decisions…

TONY. You really don't know him at all do you?

LUKE. I explained there was no pressure but he didn't believe me.

TARA. Luke's doing an amazing, amazing thing. If you understood more about dharma you'd…

TONY. I don't give a shit about 'dharma'.

TARA. I'm not a 'brainwasher', I'm just someone trying to create real happiness now and in future lives…

TONY. 'Future lives'. Jesus Christ. I can't believe you actually believe this shit.

LUKE. Okay, well, why don't you tell us your logical reasons for *not* believing in future lives and we'll tell you our reasons for?

TONY. It's called science. Haven't you heard? Science and religion had a fight, and science won.

LUKE. If it's science, you should be able to prove it.

TONY. Don't need to. I'll leave that to the scientists.

TARA. You just believe everything scientists tell you? Sort of like if you were religious and they were priests?

TONY. Nice irony. Very nice. You're ironising all over me. I'm not the one on trial here.

TARA. You're obviously suffering from a great deal of anger.

TONY. I've got a lot to be angry about. He's giving you my home.

TARA. He's not actually giving it to me, he's giving it to the centre...

TONY. And that makes you feel better about it than if he tucked a fifty into your knickers?

LUKE. Shut up!

LUKE instinctively stands up to confront TONY – *then remembers why he was sitting down. He quickly grabs the duvet behind him, pulls the whole thing off the bed, rolls it into a ball with the magazine inside and shoves it under the bed.*

(*To* TARA, *explaining.*) The duvet's, not that – clean.

TONY. He's in love with you, he's desperate to fuck you. That's why he's so keen to give you all his money. 'To have and to hold, for better for worse, for richer, for poorer...'

LUKE. That's not true.

TONY. Do you think he'd give you all his worldly goods if you were some bald sweaty fat geezer?

TARA. You're underestimating Luke's ability to...

TONY. I'm not underestimating him. Or overestimating him. I'm *estimating* him. Because I know him. A fuck's sight better than you do. He's just a pound coin with a hard-on to you, but he's my *brother*.

TARA. He's not a... we're friends. Very close friends.

TONY. You think you're saving the world, but all you're really doing is giving yourselves something to feel superior about. 'Come up to our sacred mountain and fall at our feet.' You think being a Buddhist means you're more enlightened than everyone else. All it really means is you're more fucked up, so you've grabbed a bigger bottle of medicine.

Beat.

I just want my brother back!

TARA. He's not gone anywhere. He's right here.

TONY. I want him the way he was. I want him – normal.

TARA. Don't you think it's better to be happy than to be normal?

TONY. You haven't given normal much of a chance, have you?

TARA. Look me in the eye and tell me you're happy.

TONY. Which eye? The stick-on one?

TARA realises she still has her 'third eye' on her forehead. She takes it off.

Of course I'm not happy. No one's happy. After childhood, it's a fact of life.

TARA. I'm happy. Luke's happy.

TONY. Does he look happy to you?

TARA. In general.

TONY. Yeah, sure, *in general* he's happy. Except for every minute of the day when he's fucking miserable.

Beat.

You know what? I think it's about time Tara got to know the real you…

TONY *gets the balled-up duvet from under the bed, starts opening it up.* LUKE *tries to stop him.*

LUKE. No – don't…

They struggle over the duvet.

TONY. What have you got to hide, eh? We're all friends here!

The duvet is pulled from one side by TONY *and from the other by* LUKE *– and the porn mag spills out at* TARA's *feet.*

LUKE. It's not mine.

TARA. It's fine, it's…

LUKE. It's not mine, it's his.

TONY. What?

LUKE. Tony brought it here. He – planted it on me.

TARA. It's fine, I really don't mind either way.

TONY. I can't fucking believe this. So much for the vow not to lie, eh? This is just like when Mum caught you smoking a spliff and you told her I'd 'made you do it'!

LUKE (*long, pained beat*). He's right. It's true. It is my magazine.

(*Anguished.*) I don't know why – I guess I still have a lot of, desirous attachment, I need to work on that, I'm so sorry…

TARA. You don't have to apologise to me.

TONY. Yeah, apologise to me.

TARA. My Green Tara empowerment means I'm able to transform sexual desire into wisdom. So this…

She picks up the magazine, flicks through it.

…this is just fuel to the fire of enlightenment.

TONY. You do realise you're not actually a super-being, don't you?

TARA. You do realise you're not actually Tony, don't you?

TONY. Come again?

TARA. I'm not actually Tara, you're not actually Tony, he's not actually Luke, this isn't actually a hut.

TONY. Did they put some magic mushrooms in your food box by mistake and can I have some?

TARA. It's all empty of inherent existence. It's an illusion. Whether it's a lovely illusion or a horrible one depends on whether you've got a lovely mind or a horrible one.

TONY. Like in *The Matrix*?

TARA. Sort of like in *The Matrix*.

TONY. Yeah well, I'm taking the fucking red pill.

(*To* LUKE.) Feel free to send through a revised offer by email, phone or psychic messaging.

TONY *grabs his rucksack and exits*.

LUKE (*after a beat*). I'm really sorry.

TARA. It's – okay.

(*After a beat*.) Luke?

LUKE. Yeah?

TARA. You know you're only supposed to have seven bowls?

LUKE. What?

TARA. You're only supposed to have seven bowls. You've got eight.

LUKE. Are you sure it's not eight?

TARA. It's definitely seven.

LUKE. Oh. I've always done eight.

Looks at shrine.

Oh. Oh right.

Beat.

Well, this is all a total fucking mess, isn't it?

TARA. No, it's fine, it's…

LUKE. It's not bloody fine…

LUKE *takes the extra bowl off, throws it against the wall. He pushes his face into the meditation cushion, screams into it*.

Beat.

I'm sorry… you shouldn't be seeing me like this…

TARA. Everyone loses it occasionally. Even the Dalai Lama probably kicks the cat when no one's looking.

Then:

I mean – I'm sure he doesn't, that would be terrible.

LUKE (*after a beat*). Maybe I shouldn't be getting ordained. Maybe I'm not ready?

Beat.

What do you think? Do you think I should do it?

TARA. It's your decision.

LUKE. I know, but what do you think?

TARA. It's up to you. It's your karma.

LUKE. I know it's my karma, but sometimes I don't know what my karma is.

TARA. You've got to listen to the Buddha within you.

LUKE. I know, but sometimes I wish he'd speak a bit louder, you know? So I can actually hear.

TARA. He talks the language of the heart.

LUKE. Yeah I know, but I wish he'd talk the language of the… English.

Beat.

What do you really think though? Do you think I should call it off?

TARA. Luke…

LUKE. I'm not asking you to tell me what to do.

TARA. You sort of are though?

LUKE. Yeah but I won't definitely do it. I just want to know what you think.

Beat.

Look, I've agreed to undergo brain surgery and I want
a second opinion.

TARA (*after a beat*). Okay... well... if you really want to know
what I think then I think... I think – yes. You should.

LUKE. Right. Of course. No. You're right. I can't pull out now.
I should just go through with it. Keeping your promises,
that's probably one of the vows... is it in the Bodhisattva
vows or...?

TARA. When I said yes what I meant was – yes you should call
it off.

LUKE. Oh. Oh right. Okay.

TARA. I just think you're not ready.

LUKE. Right.

TARA. It's a big commitment. It's not for everyone.

LUKE. You don't think I'm up to it.

TARA. I didn't say that.

LUKE. But that's what you think. You don't think I can pull it
off.

TARA. 'Pull it off'? Getting ordained shouldn't be like trying to
'pop a wheelie'.

Beat.

You don't have to be a monk to be a Buddhist.

LUKE. Yeah but they're the best kind of Buddhist aren't they?
The monks and the nuns, they're sort of the Buddhist – SAS.
The Elite Squadron.

TARA. Yeah but it's not the army – it's not a 'career' – you
don't have to 'go for promotion'...

LUKE. Yeah but you sort of do though don't you? Aren't we all
going for promotion – to Buddhahood?

TARA. Maybe you're just taking it a bit too seriously?

LUKE. How can you take it too seriously? It's the most important thing in the world? Isn't it?

TARA. Yes, but at the end of the day meditation's about relaxation – chilling out...

LUKE. Isn't it also about renouncing worldly life and facing up to suffering and death?

TARA. It's a bit of both?

LUKE. 'Chill out and think about death'?

TARA. I just think you need to get out of your own head. Don't take this the wrong way, but you're kind of dead from the neck down.

LUKE. What's the right way to take that?

TARA. You need to leave the ivory tower. Switch off. Eat a pizza. Watch *The Simpsons*. Have a shag.

LUKE's ears prick up.

You don't have to prove anything to anyone. You're great just the way you are.

LUKE. Thanks. I think you're great too.

Awkward beat – then:

About the temple. Tony said something... I'm sure it's just bullshit but – you do own the centre, don't you? The land?

TARA (*thrown*). Own it? Er. Well – kind of.

LUKE. You definitely told me you owned it. When you asked for the money.

TARA. I didn't 'ask for the money'. You offered it.

LUKE. When I offered it, then.

TARA (*on the back foot*). I did tell you the truth. I'd paid the deposit and was making down payments. But then the asking price changed. The wanker – I mean the guy who owns the farm – the farmer – he saw how popular the centre was getting and doubled his price.

LUKE. Right.

TARA. I should have told you. I just didn't want to – bother you with all that – money stuff.

LUKE. But you still wanted me to give you the money.

TARA. Yes, because if you didn't I'd lose the centre.

LUKE. So the money isn't for the temple, it's to buy the centre.

TARA. No. I mean, yes. I still want to build the temple. But if there's no centre, there's no temple. And if I don't get a guarantor in ten days' time there won't be – anything.

LUKE. Ten days?? And that's me, is it? I'm the guarantor?

She doesn't respond.

Of course I am.

TARA. Now can you see why I didn't tell you? If you'd changed your mind, everything would be over!

LUKE. What about the contract? He can't just change the terms…

TARA. We don't have a contract. As such. Well, we did, but it was – a verbal contract.

LUKE. A verbal contract?

TARA. The whole point of this place is to get away from contracts and rules and regulations and all that shit.

LUKE. This is a great illustration of why contracts and rules and regulations can actually be a really good idea.

TARA. All right, 'Dad'.

LUKE. You want 'Dad' to buy you a retreat centre but you don't want 'Dad' to get all hardass about the terms and conditions?

TARA (*after a beat*). I had this amazing vision from White Tara in my meditation last night. She was floating down from the God realm on her wish-fulfilling wheel and this teardrop of compassion fell from her eye on to the earth and this amazing beautiful crystal temple sprang up!

LUKE. It's a shame she didn't weep tears of money into your bank account while she was at it.

Beat.

Look – I didn't sign up to be some kind of saviour for the whole centre…

TARA. Sure.

Trying to be strong and cool.

It's – your decision.

LUKE. Although it's pretty obvious what you want my decision to be.

TARA. Whether you use your money to save the centre and build an amazing jewel sending out infinite rays of healing light to the universe, or just keep your money for yourself – it's entirely up to you.

LUKE. Thanks for that.

TARA. All I'd say is… there are a lot of people who've resigned their jobs and uprooted their lives to come and live here.

LUKE. I didn't tell them to do that.

TARA. We've bought some really big saucepans. I've got all these massive pans. It's entirely up you, but the pans are fucking huge.

LUKE. Oh right, the pans, the pans, I'm so sorry I made you waste so much money on so many enormous pans!

TARA (*after a beat*). I should go.

TARA *turns to exit.*

LUKE. Don't.

Beat.

You know, when we first met at the festival I thought
everyone was a bit weird, apart from you.

TARA. Er, well, thanks.

Beat.

But like all phenomena, I'm empty of inherent existence.

LUKE. Well, of all phenomena that are empty of inherent
existence, you're my favourite.

Beat.

It was so weird, the way we met. I hadn't split up from Lisa
that long and… I sometimes think of how different things
might have been. Between us.

Beat.

I guess we missed our chance. Or – maybe now's our
chance? Our second chance?

TARA. How do you mean?

LUKE. There's still a month to go before I'm meant to take my
vows. Maybe we should – kick the tyres?

TARA. Kick the what?

LUKE *goes in for a kiss.*

LUKE (*breaking off – then*). Sorry, I shouldn't have… that
was…

TARA. No, er, it's – okay.

LUKE. If you want you can – spend the night?

TARA. Uh… well… Can we just – maybe – see how it goes?

LUKE. You mean – see if I come through with the million quid
or not?

TARA. That's not what I meant.

LUKE. If I gave you the million, would you spend the night?

TARA *hesitates.*

What do you reckon? Million quid and a Buddhist centre in exchange for one disappointing shag?

TARA. Are you making an 'indecent proposal'?

LUKE. I'm joking. Forget about the money. Let's just…

LUKE *goes towards* TARA, *she backs away.*

TARA. I'm sorry, Luke, I don't think…

LUKE. Right. No. Sure. I'm sorry.

Beat.

So that's that then.

TARA. What's – what?

LUKE. It's never going to happen between us.

TARA. Luke. I did like you. I *do* like you. But it was only a few months after we met you said you wanted to become a monk.

LUKE. Yeah but you've got a point – about me not being ready.

TARA. So now you want to stop being a monk so we can fuck?

LUKE. No. I mean – unless – do you want to?

TARA. Who are you, Luke? How am I supposed to know who you are when you've clearly got no bloody idea?

LUKE. I'm sorry, this isn't what I… this is all a big mess. I thought you meant… you were the one saying, about watching *The Simpsons* and having a shag…?

TARA. I didn't necessarily mean me. I meant – a, general shag.

LUKE. Right. Of course. General, shagging.

TARA. Like I didn't specifically mean *The Simpsons*. I meant you could watch anything light-hearted. *Family Guy. Anchorman.*

LUKE. *Anchorman?*

TARA. Don't tell me you've never seen *Anchorman?*

The door opens and a wet and bedraggled TONY *appears.*

TONY. It's fucking great, *Anchorman*.

Takes off his wet coat.

Started pissing down so I thought fuck it, I'll go back in the morning.

LUKE *turns away from them both, goes to the shrine, starts tidying up.*

You two look like you've been having a 'big chat'.

TARA. I should go.

LUKE. Just so you know. I'm going to keep my money. And my flat.

LUKE *finishes putting the candles and offering bowls back. He gets out his meditation cushion.*

TARA. So that's – it?

LUKE. That's it.

TONY. So you're not kicking me out then?

LUKE. No.

TONY. Sorry, sweetheart. Family comes first. Fuck you, and fuck all the Buddhists.

LUKE. That's obviously not what I'm saying.

TARA. Right. You do realise that without the money the centre is going to close?

LUKE. Just because I don't choose to save someone's life doesn't make me a murderer. It's not my fault you didn't sign a contract.

TARA. I'm not saying it is. Just…

LUKE. I'm sure you'll sort out some kind of – arrangement.

TARA. I've tried. We won't.

TONY. I bet you're having second thoughts about not putting out for him now, aren't you? The million-pound hand job? Yeah, I was listening.

TARA. Fuck off.

(*To* LUKE.) You're choosing this arsehole over me, and the centre and – everything?

LUKE *sits on the cushion in meditation posture.*

LUKE. I'm not 'choosing' him. Or anyone.

LUKE *closes his eyes, commences meditation.*

TARA. Right. Well. Have a great rest of your retreat.

TONY (*unfriendly*). Bye bye!

TARA *gives* TONY *the finger and exits.*

All right if I stay the night?

LUKE. Sure. You can have the bed, I'll sleep on the floor.

TONY. It's your bed. I should sleep on the floor.

Beat – then:

Actually the floor is pretty fucking hard. Maybe I will take the bed.

TONY *crosses, sits on the bed.*

LUKE (*opens his eyes*). Why don't you do some meditation with me?

TONY. Nah, I don't need to meditate. I'm already chilled. To the max.

LUKE. If you're so chilled, why is it you can't sit still for just a few seconds?

TONY. I could if I want to, I just don't feel like it.

LUKE. Sure.

TONY. I could meditate your head off. I could meditate better than you doing a bungee jump with a feather duster up my arse.

LUKE. Go on then.

TONY. All right. Let's have it. You and me. A meditation-off.

LUKE. Great.

Beat.

Okay. So just close your eyes. And allow your body to relax. Now, let's begin by visualising that sitting in front of us is Buddha himself. And around us, under his compassionate gaze, are our family, our friends, our acquaintances…

Beat.

Now we can extend our visualisation to include all the sentient beings in the world, not just humans but animals too…

TONY. What, like all the ants in the world?

LUKE. Er, yes, but if it's easier, you can imagine them in human form…

TONY. Imagine I'm surrounded by billions of ants the size of people?

LUKE. Not human-*size* ants – ants in human *form*…

TONY. Tiny ant-men? I thought this was supposed be relaxing?

LUKE. Let's move on to the breathing meditation. Just become aware of the breath as it gently enters and leaves the body. If you get distracted by any thoughts, gently let go of them and return your attention very naturally to the breath.

They sit silently for a beat.

TONY. Can't we put some music on?

LUKE. Uh… not really.

TONY. I've got a better idea – how about I lead a meditation – a fun meditation?

LUKE. But you've never actually… I mean you don't know how to…

TONY. Come on, you've had your go, it was rubbish, now it's my turn.

Beat.

Right. So. Imagine you're sitting on a velvet cushion on a diamond throne in, like – a palace made of chocolate. Yeah?

LUKE *crosses to the kitchen area, fills his offering jug with water. Then he returns to the shrine and carefully fills the offering bowls. When he finishes, he picks up his mala.*

The castle starts to melt and the cushion transforms into a magical windsurfer and you're surfing through the sky, and Harry Hill and Will Smith are surfing through the sky with you. Then these three gorgeous chicks windsurf up – a blonde, a redhead and a brunette – wearing skintight gold bodysuits. The brunette comes up to Will Smith and asks him where he wants to go and he says 'Tahiti' and they whizz off together. Then the redhead goes up to Harry Hill and Harry says 'Debenhams' cos he's making a joke, and they whizz off together. Then the blonde comes up to you and you say 'Superman's Fortress of Solitude' and she says 'That's fictional' and you say 'You didn't say it had to be real' and she says 'It was implied' and you say 'No it wasn't' and she starts to look annoyed but you can tell she's loving the banter. Then she whizzes up into space and you chase after her and you chase her across the moon towards this enormous bouncy castle. And inside the bouncy castle are all these gorgeous film stars and models, and they're all naked and oiled and bouncing up and down, and their tits are bouncing up and down, and the blonde chick is laughing and she strips off her gold suit and dives in and starts bouncing all over Beyoncé and Scarlett Johansson...

LUKE. Tony. Are you getting a hard-on?

TONY. Kind of. Just a bit of a semi.

LUKE. You're not supposed to get a hard-on when you're meditating.

TONY. Who says? Why not?

TONY *lies down on the bed, gets comfortable. After a beat he picks up a Buddhist book from the side table, starts to read.*

Are we going back to London then? The old team, back together?

LUKE. I don't know. Maybe. Let's see.

LUKE *rings the singing bowl and picks up the mala.*

Om mani padme hum – Om mani padme hum – Om mani padme hum

After a beat TONY *chucks the Buddhist book on to the floor and picks up the porn mag.*

End.

A Nick Hern Book

The Retreat first published in Great Britain as a paperback original in 2017 by
Nick Hern Books Limited, The Glasshouse, 49a Goldhawk Road, London
W12 8QP, in association with Debbie Hicks Productions, Park Theatre, London,
and the King's Head Theatre, London

The Retreat copyright © 2017 Sam Bain

Sam Bain has asserted his right to be identified as the author of this work

Cover image: Rebecca Pitt Creative

Designed and typeset by Nick Hern Books, London
Printed in Great Britain by Mimeo Ltd, Huntingdon, Cambridgeshire PE29 6XX

A CIP catalogue record for this book is available from the British Library

ISBN   978 1 84842 688 7